24

season 2

Pass me on when
you've finished
reading me
Healthy
Planet
www.healthyplanet.org

24

season 2

The Unofficial Guide

Mark Wright

First published 2003 by Contender Books
Contender Books is a division of
The Contender Entertainment Group
48 Margaret Street
London
W1W 8SE

This edition published 2003

1 3 5 7 9 10 8 6 4 2

ISBN 1 84357 072 6

Printed in the UK by Butler & Tanner Ltd, Frome and London
Cover design: Burville-Riley
Text design and typesetting: seagulls
Edited by Wendy Hollas
Production by Sasha Morton

This is a work of critical review, based on episodes from the television series *24* which have been broadcast in the UK on terrestrial and satellite channels. This is not an official *24* product and has not been endorsed by the programme makers.

ACKNOWLEDGEMENTS

Thanks go on this one, in no particular order: the gang down at the Mei Chuan Euston Massive – Barry, Janet, Pete and Shazza; the Notplayers for much needed (in)sanity; Cav Scott, Gary Russell, Bob Curbishley, Wendy Albiston, Daniel Brennan, Sam Green, Zoe, Jason Haigh-Ellery for allowing the Tomorrow People to be less than punctual, Matt Dobson for making sure our heart rates were correct; Lennie James for handing me the Barbie Twins and the Man from Del Monte on a plate; David Cox at DSA; Zara Lansdale, Tamzin Sylvester and the team at *Pure 24*

As always, there are those without whom...

Mike Ward – he knows why; James White for the Dennis Haysbert interview; Jac Rayner for proofing the book when she was tied up with werewolves; Clayton Hickman for putting up with a loony flatmate throughout; Lee Binding for lunch, laughs, larks and for letting me play with *The Professionals*; Michele Brown; Sasha Morton for putting up with me once more above and beyond the call and soothing a much fevered brow; Jim Sangster for keeping me supplied with episodes – the curry and beer's on me fellah; and finally, Alison Parker, who took me on as her 'new project' and kept me plied with red wine and chunky chips when needed most. Life's a winner! And of course, the cast and crew of *24* for providing the best television entertainment around. Cheers guys!

24 Hours Party People

OK, so it's an obvious gag, but the title of this introduction is, nevertheless, apt. After the success garnered by the first, award-winning series of *24*, the party must have lasted *at least* 24 hours. However, creators Robert Cochran and Joel Surnow probably went to bed early, having the daunting task of planning the second season of a show that had provided enough water-cooler conversations to last a lifetime. And here we are, tuning in for another slice of the ultimate bad day.

Jim Sangster, author of the first volume of *24: The Unofficial Guide*, posed an obvious question in his summing up of Season One's closing episode: '...how can Series Two possibly top that?' How indeed. When you've pushed a man to the very limits of endurance, deprived him of sleep and food, kidnapped his family, tied him up, blown him up, shot at him, and finally taken away a loved one in a horribly violent fashion, where else can you push him? I don't know, but it's going to be fun finding out. Back to that water cooler on Monday morning...

This second volume of *24: The Unofficial Guide* will take you, hour by hour, minute by minute, through the ins and outs of the second season. Kiefer Sutherland is back as Jack Bauer, and Dennis

Haysbert returns as Palmer, now the President of the United States. There are some other familiar faces around, along with new personnel at the Counter Terrorist Unit, and this book will be your guide to the characters and the convoluted events as they unfold. Some categories are the same as before, and there are a few new ones. The episode summaries will break down as follows:

EPISODE TITLE

Production Code: The code assigned by the production team for each episode.

Writer/Director Credits.

Guest Cast: All credited actors aside from the regulars.

FIELD REPORT

A detailed breakdown of the events of each episode, with time checks where appropriate.

CTU INCIDENT REPORT

Haven't I Seen You Somewhere Before?: A rundown of where you might have seen a guest actor before.

Behind The Camera: Notes on the career of that particular episode's writer(s) and director.

Time Checks: When characters remind each other of when something happened, or when it's going to happen – a writer's tool to push home the 'real-time' aspect of the show.

Fashion Police: The fashion triumphs and disasters, and notes of when characters deign to change their clothes during the course of the day.

The Perils Of Kim: She might look great in skimpy shorts, but Kim Bauer shows a staggering talent for getting herself into hot water and an even more staggering talent for not doing the right thing to get out of it. Find out just how dumb she's been this week.

It's Not Easy Being Jack: Jack Bauer is not a man you want to mess with, and here we'll tell you why.

Great Lines: Any notable or quote-worthy lines from the episode.

Death Count: A running tally of the body count as it mounts up over the 24 weeks.

Trivia: Anything we can think of!

DEBRIEF

A summing-up of the episode's strengths and weaknesses, along with some discussion of a related theme.

Pulse Rate: Were our hearts pumping for this one? With 100 bpm as a resting heart rate, the better the episode, the faster that blood pumps!

Questions Arising: Finally, some of the questions that have been posed during the episode and are unanswered by the end. Will they be resolved, or will they be lost in favour of forward plotting?

Some things will doubtless be missed along the way – a line here, a trivial plot moment there, but hopefully I've managed to get in just about everything that makes *24* such a unique television show. And, if I've missed your favourite bit, you could always have my family kidnapped and force me to assassinate a president!

Mark Wright
London, June 2003

Personnel Files

THE CHARACTERS

Jack Bauer

Jack Bauer is a contradiction. On the one hand he is a ruthless military man who you would never want to mess with, prepared to do anything it takes to get the job done. Jack's tendency to act first, think later, puts him into conflict with his superiors and often places colleagues in difficult positions or even danger. On the other hand, he is compassionate, loyal to those around him, and a loving family man. Jack's military career, which began with a stint in the Los Angeles Police Department Special Weapons and Tactics (SWAT) team, has often conflicted with his commitment to family. Before joining the Counter Terrorist Unit as Special Agent in Charge, Jack was the commander of Operation Nightfall, authorised by Senator David Palmer and intended to eliminate Kosovan war criminal Victor Drazen. Although Drazen's wife and daughter were killed, Drazen himself, unknown to Jack, was brought to the United States. In a subsequent attempt by Drazen's sons to assassinate Palmer and discredit Bauer, Jack's wife, Teri, died at the hands of his former mistress, Nina Myers.

Since Teri's death and the events surrounding the assassination plot, Jack has left his position at CTU. He is estranged from daughter Kimberley and struggling to get his life back together.

President David Palmer

David Palmer is the first African-American to become President of the United States. A former Attorney at Law, Palmer's experience in politics is extensive, having acted as both a Representative and Senator in the United States Congress. It was while acting as a member of the Senate Appropriations Committee that he approved Operation Nightfall, designed to eliminate Victor Drazen.

The events surrounding his attempted assassination during the Californian presidential primary elections put a great strain on David Palmer and his family. Although he remains close to his children, Keith and Nicole, he is now divorced from his wife, Sherry.

Kimberly Bauer

Kimberly 'Kim' Bauer is the only child of Jack Bauer and Teri Bauer (deceased). During her parents' brief separation shortly before Teri's death, Kim took the side of her father, which caused the rift between Kim and her mother to widen. The rift healed somewhat during the period in which they were kidnapped by Ira Gaines, acting under instructions from the Drazen family.

Kim is having a better time dealing with Teri's death than her father seems to be, although in the 18 months since the events of Day One father and daughter have barely spoken. Kim dropped out of high school before matriculation, and is working as a nanny for the Matheson family, looking after their daughter Megan.

Kate Warner

Kate Warner is the eldest daughter of wealthy businessman Robert Warner. Her younger sister, Marie, is due to wed Reza Naiyeer, who has been working for the family company. Suspicious of her sister's fiancé, Kate has had a background check carried out by a private investigator. Although Reza's personal file is clean, his name comes up in connection with a known terrorist.

Tony Almeida

Prior to working as a senior intelligence agent at the Los Angeles Domestic Unit of CTU, Tony Almeida gained the rank of First Lieutenant in the US Marines. He is a capable sniper and expert in hand-to-hand combat, and also possesses skills in computer science and engineering.

Tony worked closely with Jack Bauer on Operation Proteus, for which he received a commendation. Although he had feelings for former colleague Nina Myers, Tony denies any liaison ever took place between them. He was, however, jealous of Myers's affair with Bauer, which put a strain on his relationship with his superior. Since the events of Day One, Tony appears to be the only operative within CTU whom Jack Bauer will trust.

George Mason

George Mason is currently the Special Agent in Charge of the Los Angeles Domestic Unit of CTU, taking over the position vacated by Jack Bauer, which would appear to be a demotion. Prior to this, Mason held a number of senior positions within CTU, rising to Senior Section Leader of the Washington headquarters.

Mason is ambitious, cowardly and thoroughly political in everything he does. He is divorced and estranged from his son.

Sherry Palmer

Sherry Palmer missed out on being First Lady of America when she betrayed her husband during the California primaries. Shortly afterwards, David Palmer divorced her, although she maintains that her actions were motivated by a need to protect her family.

Sherry and David were childhood sweethearts, and throughout her husband's presidential campaign she was his most eager supporter. Her ruthlessness shows that she may have a greater understanding of politics than her ex-husband.

Michelle Dessler

Michelle Dessler has been with CTU for around six months, and as the unit's Internet Protocol Manager she is highly skilled in all areas of computer science. She appears disciplined and determined, carrying herself with an efficient air.

As a relatively new member of the CTU team, nobody knows exactly where Michelle's loyalties lie, although it seems fair to say that she thinks Tony Almeida is hot (but who doesn't?).

Paula Schaeffer

Paula Schaeffer is the newest recruit to the duty roster at CTU, hired as a computer programmer, a position previously held by the deceased Jamey Farrell. Paula was brought into the agency by Tony Almeida and is enthusiastic, eager to please, and over the moon to be working for her country.

THE ACTORS

Kiefer Sutherland [Jack Bauer]

'I wanted to spend more time with my daughter, and *24* offered me a chance to be in LA for at least eight months.'

Kiefer Sutherland is perhaps one of the most underrated actors to emerge from the so-called 'brat pack' of the late 1980s. Alongside Charlie Sheen, Emilio Esteves, Oliver Platt, Christian Slater, Julia Roberts and Lou Diamond Phillips, Sutherland was a well-known name in films throughout the late 1980s and early 1990s. By the end of the decade, although still working steadily, his name was all but forgotten.

Then came a show called *24*.

The success of *24* is arguably responsible for the upturn in Kiefer Sutherland's fortunes as a Hollywood star. Older, wiser perhaps, he is no longer the pretty boy hellraiser with a well-publicised split from

Julia Roberts dragging his name into the tabloids. Jack Bauer has enabled Sutherland to take his deserved place as a fine character actor, and the audience want more.

Kiefer Sutherland was born on 18 December 1966 in London, England, and christened Kiefer William Frederick Dempsey George Rufus Sutherland. He was named after Warren Kiefer, the pseudonym of Lorenzo Sabatini. Sabatini directed 1964's *Il Castello Dei Morti Vivi* (*Castle of the Living Dead*) in which Kiefer's father, Donald Sutherland, made his feature film debut. After the breakup of her marriage, Sutherland's mother, actress Shirley Douglas, raised Kiefer and his twin sister Rachel in her native Canada.

At the age of 15, Kiefer dropped out of high school to begin his early flirtation with acting. His feature film debut came in 1983 with the Matthew Broderick vehicle *Max Dugan Returns*, which coincidentally also starred father Donald. Kiefer eventually landed a role in an episode of *Steven Spielberg's Amazing Stories* in 1985, although he began to make his mark with a memorable turn in Rob Reiner's *Stand By Me* (1986).

Sutherland's star really started to shine in 1986, when director Joel Schumacher cast him as David, the edgy leader of a pack of vampires in *The Lost Boys*. Around the same time, while working on *The Killing Time* (1987), Kiefer met his first wife, producer Camelia Cath, 14 years his senior. They married in 1988, but the marriage lasted just two years.

In the meantime, Sutherland's career was in the ascendance, with starring roles in *Bright Lights, Big City* (1988), *1969* (1988), *Promised Land* (1988) and the box-office smash, *Young Guns* (1988). The western teamed him with Emilio Esteves and *24* guest star Lou Diamond Phillips.

A sequel to *Young Guns* came in 1990, along with a reunion with director Joel Schumacher for the film *Flatliners*. During filming, Sutherland began a romance with co-star Julia Roberts, and the couple were set to wed on 14 June 1991. Sadly it was not to be, with

Roberts absconding to Europe with Sutherland's friend and *The Lost Boys* co-star Jason Patric.

The next few years would see Kiefer busier than ever, managing to squeeze in roles in *Article 99* (1992), *Twin Peaks: Fire Walk With Me* (1992), *A Few Good Men* (1992), *The Vanishing* (1993) and the brat pack spin on *The Three Musketeers* (1993). A third teaming with Joel Schumacher came in 1996 for the John Grisham adaptation, *A Time To Kill.*

Although by no means as prolific, the second half of the decade saw Sutherland making some interesting choices, most notably the eerily satisfying *Dark City* (1998). In 1993, Sutherland made his directorial debut with the TV movie *Last Light*, followed up by the feature films *Truth Or Consequences, N.M.* (1997) and *Woman Wanted* (1999). His second marriage, to Kelly Winn, ended in 2000 after four years.

Since the success of *24*, Kiefer Sutherland is once again in demand, although the demands of a TV series schedule limit his choices of projects. He has been seen in *Desert Saints* (2002) and *Behind The Red Door* (2002), in a fourth collaboration with Joel Schumacher, *Phone Booth* (2002), and he also gave a well-received turn as artist Paul Gauguin in the otherwise average *Paradise Found* (2002).

Aside from his acting commitments, Kiefer Sutherland is a keen ice hockey player with a regular place on a celebrity team, and in the late 1990s toured on the rodeo circuit, with wins in Phoenix and Alburquerque, and first place in the U.S. Team Roping Championships. Trivia fans may like to know that his grandfather, Tommy Douglas, was the first elected socialist Prime Minister of Canada. He is 5'10".

As well as playing the lead role of Jack Bauer in *24*, Sutherland also acts as a producer on the series.

Dennis Haysbert [President David Palmer]

'He's a president on national television, in a three-dimensional role, who exemplifies integrity and dignity. You don't see a lot of roles like that for anybody, much less an American actor of African descent. Now we'll see how long it is before society catches up with TV.'

Even before the second series of *24* had completed its run on American TV, Dennis Haysbert had been nominated for a Golden Globe award for his role as President David Palmer. Clocking in at an impressive 6'4", Dennis Dexter Haysbert nearly missed out on an acting career, but chose to decline numerous sports scholarships to attend the American Academy of Dramatic Arts. Since he made his television debut in an episode of the highly acclaimed *Lou Grant* in the late 1970s, Haysbert has rarely been off our screens, both silver and small. Among Haysbert's extensive TV guest credits are some of America's most popular shows – *Quincy*, *Buck Rogers in the 25th Century*, *The Incredible Hulk*, *Laverne and Shirley*, *The Fall Guy*, *The A Team*, *Magnum P.I.* and *Scarecrow and Mrs King*. He has also lent his distinctive vocal talent to the animated adventures of *Batman*, *Justice League* and *Duckman*. He played the regular character of Dr Theodore Morris in the short-lived *Now and Again*.

Haysbert's film credits are just as extensive as his work in television. He made his big screen debut in *Major League* (1989) with Charlie Sheen, and returned for both sequels. He went on to appear in *Heat* (1995), *Waiting To Exhale* (1995), *Insomnia* (1996), *Absolute Power* (1997), *Random Hearts* (1999) and *The Thirteenth Floor* (1999). Since finding wider acclaim in *24*, Haysbert has taken on the role of Raymond Deagan in Todd Haynes' *Far From Heaven* (2002), playing opposite Julianne Moore.

Haysbert has two daughters and is a strong campaigner in the fight against AIDS.

Elisha Cuthbert [Kim Bauer]

'She's a lot stronger this year and I want people to see that she's actually Kiefer's daughter and not just anyone's daughter. He's in the CIA and she's got to be tough too.'

Elisha Ann Cuthbert was born on 30 November 1982 in Calgary, Canada and began her showbusiness career as a model at the age of seven. In 1997, Elisha became a globetrotting correspondent for the Canadian children's TV series *Popular Mechanics for Kids.* During this time, she came to the attention of Hilary Clinton, who just happened to be married to the President of the United States, and Elisha was invited to Washington for a meeting with the First Lady.

Acting did not form part of Cuthbert's CV until she spent the day as an extra on the spooky kids' horror series *Are You Afraid of the Dark?*, and was delighted to be invited back as a series regular a few years later. Having been well and truly bitten by the acting bug, Elisha clocked up roles in the films *Dancing On The Moon* (1998), *Nico The Unicorn* (1998) and *Airspeed* (1998).

At the age of 17, Cuthbert moved to Los Angeles, where she has lived ever since. 'I was lucky,' she has said of her acting career, 'I found what I wanted to do when I was 11.' Since her casting as Kim Bauer in *24* in 2001, Elisha has become something of a pin-up, featuring on the covers of men's lifestyle magazines, including *FHM*. Her film roles since *24* have included the successful comedy *Old School* (2003), starring Vince Vaughan, and the lead in the forthcoming *The Girl Next Door* (2003).

Elisha's nickname is Heesh.

Sarah Wynter [Kate Warner]

'I just always wanted to act. It started out as a fantasy, just wanting to be other people. Now I feel like I have the fantasy job of all time.'

Born on 15 February 1973, Australian born Sarah Wynter moved to New York City to study drama at the Penny Templeton Studio when she was 17. After graduating she went on to appear in several off-Broadway productions, before making her screen debut as Sara in the romantic drama *Let It Be* (1995), which was followed by a minor role in *Species II* three years later.

Following her early film work, Sarah won roles in *Molly* (1999), *Farewell, My Love* (1999), *Lost Souls* (2000) with Ben Chaplin and Winona Ryder, *Jerks* (2000), *Bride Of The Wind* (2001), *Coastlines* (2002) and *Moving August* (2002). She also had a guest role in the pilot episode of *Sex and the City* in 1988. She is perhaps best known as deadly Russian assassin Talia Elsworth in the Arnold Schwarzenegger action movie, *The 6th Day* (2000).

Xander Berkeley [George Mason]

'It's good to not feel like the work you're doing is some fluff entertainment that's about diversionary denial, but it gets to be a bit intense when it seems like it's reflecting so actively events that are taking place in the world.'

Xander Berkeley's extensive career as an actor stretches back over twenty years to his TV debut as a marine in a 1981 episode of *M*A*S*H.* Since then he has clocked up more than 30 film appearances and guest-starred in numerous television shows. Aside from appearing in TV shows such as *Hart to Hart*, *Remington Steele*, *The A Team*, *Moonlighting* and *Miami Vice*, he is also a noted voice artist, having worked on *Gargoyles*, *The Wild Thornberries*, *Duckman* and *Batman Beyond*. He has also found time to devote to the theatre, spending a period acting in off-Broadway productions and regional theatre, including Shakespearean roles. He is a keen sculptor and painter.

Xander Berkeley's film credits include *Sid And Nancy* (1986), *The Fabulous Baker Boys* (1989), *Internal Affairs* (1990), *Terminator 2* (1991), *A Few Good Men* (1992) with Kiefer Sutherland, *Apollo 13* (1995), *Heat* (1995) alongside Dennis Haysbert, *Air Force One* (1997) and *Shanghai Noon* (2000).

On 7 September 2002, Xander Berkeley's connection to *24* took on a more personal tone when he married co-star Sarah Clarke (Nina Myers).

Carlos Bernard [Tony Almeida]

'When I go through traumatic experiences, get burned or whatever it is, my reaction is to shed things – cut my hair, get rid of stuff, shave, try to leave as much behind as I can stand and start anew, try to move forward.'

Born in Chicago, Carlos Bernard Papierski studied acting in San Francisco, graduating with a Masters degree in Fine Arts from the American Conservatory Theatre. He has spent much of his career in the theatre, remaining with the American Conservatory Theatre to appear in *Good* with William Hurt, *Hamlet*, *As You Like It*, and *The Cherry Orchard*.

Bernard has guest starred on television in *Babylon 5*, *Walker, Texas Ranger*, and *Silk Stalkings*, as well as being a regular in the popular U.S. daytime soap *The Young and the Restless.* His film appearances include *The Killing Jar* (1996), *Mars And Beyond* (2000) and *The Colonel's Last Flight* (2000). Fans of Carlos should check out his official website at http://carlosbernard.com.

Penny Johnson Jerald [Sherry Palmer]

'I just said, "Oh, who's playing the husband?" and they said, "Dennis Haysbert" and I said, "Oh, yeah, I want to do this!" Dennis and I have been husband and wife before.'

Penny Johnson's desire to become an actress was so great that at the age of 13 she lied to gain entry to the Center Stage Theatre of Baltimore who held workshops for teenagers aged 14 and above.

Johnson performed mime, juggling and even fire-eating with the Theatre Project, and before starting her lengthy career as an actress studied the Suzuki Method of classical music in Japan and attended the Juilliard School.

Penny Johnson's TV credits are numerous, having appeared in everything from *Hill Street Blues* to *The X-Files*. She has had roles in films including *What's Love Got To Do With It* (1993) and *Absolute Power* (1997) with her *24* screen husband, Dennis Haysbert. She also played the recurring role of Nurse Practitioner Lynette Evans in several episodes of *ER*.

Prior to *24*, Johnson was best known on television for two very different roles. She gained a nomination for an NAACP Image Award for her role as the long-suffering Beverley Barnes in *The Larry Sanders Show*, and for four years she played Captain Cassidy Yates, the ongoing love interest for Captain Benjamin Sisko in *Star Trek: Deep Space Nine*.

Behind the Scenes

Joel Surnow

[Creator/Writer/Executive Producer]

Along with *24*'s co-creator Robert Cochran, Joel Surnow won an Emmy award for Outstanding Writing on a Drama Series for the pilot episode of *24*. Prior to creating *24*, Surnow had been executive producer on the popular *La Femme Nikita*, and his previous TV credits include writer and producer duties on *The Equaliser*, *Wiseguy*, *Nowhere Man*, *The Commish* and *Miami Vice*.

Robert Cochran

[Creator/Writer/Executive Producer]

Robert Cochran began his career as a lawyer, making him an ideal candidate for writing legal-based drama series such as *L.A. Law*. Before putting Jack Bauer through hell in *24*, Cochran collaborated with Joel Surnow on *La Femme Nikita* and *The Commish*, and was a producer on *Falcon Crest*.

Howard Gordon

[Writer/Executive Producer]

Howard Gordon is a three-times Golden Globe winner and multi-Emmy nominee, with a career in genre television production that stretches back to the first series of *The X-Files*, a series he remained with as a senior writer and executive producer until 1998. While working on *The X-Files*, Gordon also acted as a supervising producer for 20th Century Fox's other cult television hits *Buffy the Vampire Slayer* and its spin-off *Angel*.

Brian Grazer

[Executive Producer]

At the 2002 Academy Awards, Brian Grazer walked away with an Oscar for Best Picture for Ron Howard's *A Beautiful Mind* (2002), starring Russell Crowe. As a producer, Grazer has more than 20 years of experience in Hollywood, having previously overseen production on box-office hits *Spies Like Us* (1985), *Parenthood* (1989), *Kindergarten Cop* (1990), *Ransom* (1996), *Apollo 13* (1995) and *How The Grinch Stole Christmas* (2000). Many of these projects were directed by his friend and business partner Ron Howard.

On television, Brian Grazer has been behind such hits as *Felicity*, *Sports Night* and the acclaimed Emmy-award-winning mini-series, *From the Earth to the Moon*.

In Conversation

with Dennis Haysbert

Dennis Haysbert visited London during the summer of 2002 to promote the UK DVD release of *24* and was happy to talk about the rigours of filming the first series.

What are the challenges involved in making a show as unusual as *24*?
It's a very unique challenge, but it's also pretty easy because it does happen in one day, so you don't have to worry about what clothes you're wearing – you only have to worry about your haircut, which has to stay consistent. I think they did pretty well with that. It's actually what an actor lives for – true moment-to-moment acting and even if it's across the span of a couple of days' shooting, it's still going A-Z.

But how does that affect continuity?
The lady that deals with that, our script supervisor, has to keep track of a lot of that and Tracy (Zigler), the script supervisor – she was wonderful.

Was there ever a nightmare for you where she's saying: 'Oh my god! You've changed this or that'...?
That rarely happens because we're all really aware of what we're doing and when we're doing it. You help out as best you can.

Was each episode shot as one block?
We shot two episodes at a time and so that necessitated us working six days out of every 16 days. It was eight days an episode so 16 days for two. And because it's all happening in one day, the locations don't really change that much, except for Kiefer, because he's always running around.

You do a little movement yourself – parking lot meetings etc.
I got out of the box a couple of times (laughs)...

***24* gives the impression of being one big story, but then you realise it's split into smaller sections...**
There are subsections. Every episode really does stand on its own. And then there's that through-line, that thread connecting to the next one, that turns into a rope that turns into a thick cable that turns into a wall that (smacks fists together) brings it all together.

How has *24* impacted on your career? You've done film, theatre, TV. This has been a real hit. Has it lead to opportunities?
There's a lot more interest in my motion picture career and television work, but since we've gone on for a second season, all those things will have to wait.

Any plans for the hiatus?
I have a movie coming out in November that I shot during the series last year. It's called *Far From Heaven*. Todd Haynes directing, Julianne Moore and Dennis Quaid starring.

How does that work? You're in most episodes.
With the schedule – shooting two episodes at a time, you only work those six days, which leaves you ten days to shoot other projects.

When will you rest?
I'll sleep in the break…

That must be a tough schedule – keeping your mind on where you are in the movie, and then going back to the show…
I've done repertory theatre, I'm used to all that.

How does acting on television differ from film?
Film takes you about four months to shoot, so you have a lot of time to get the character. A lot more so than television. On TV you pretty much have to pick up the character quickly, then over the course of the season it gets richer.

But the screen time's different – TV tends to be better.
The acting challenge is pretty comfortable in both cases.

How did the producers originally pitch *24* to you?
I'll tell you something – it was very easy to get me interested in this show. They told me that this guy was a senator with a good chance of becoming president. That's pretty much all I needed to know. And that that would have ramifications for his family. He had a dark secret, and there's nothing more compelling than that, so I just embraced that and worked with it.

Did they give you any indication of where the series was going, beyond the presidential possibility?
They didn't map it out. They had a bible. And they shot two endings.

Does it ever annoy you that you're trying to create this suspense and then people publish the information?
That's why I love the way this show is done because you can't do that. Because as soon as you say, 'this is what's going to happen next', they'll switch endings on you. So the misdirection on the show has been great.

After 11 September, a lot of entertainment changed. How was *24* affected?
It didn't change. The only thing they did was delete a scene with a plane explosion.

Was there any sense of panic at the time?
I think it was just time sensitive and had to be sensitive to the events of September 11.

How do you see real politicians having played one on TV?
They work hard. They're under a lot of scrutiny. And some are very, very good. Very clean. Good public servants. But a lot are dirty. It's a dirty business. Some dirt's always going to get on them. Palmer's a good man, but he's being brought down by his family and the people that are backing him.

Did you base the character on any real-life politico?
No one really. I pretty much do the role the way I want to. I do have my heroes, though – people I look up to. Bill Clinton being one of them, his mistakes not withstanding. When all's said and done, people will see him as one of our greatest presidents. And Jimmy Carter, Roosevelt. I was just reading his biography.

And you're not a big fan of the current administration?
I plead the Fifth! (laughs)

Interview conducted by James White in London, July 2002

In Conversation

with Leslie Hope

Leslie Hope played the put-upon damsel-in-distress Teri Bauer in Season One of *24* and, unless you've been on the moon or, worse, not seen the first season, you'll know that Teri doesn't make it to the cast of Season Two. While promoting the DVD release of *24* Season One on DVD in July 2002, Leslie was happy to talk about her experiences of filming *24*...

Teri gets treated very badly throughout the first season of *24*...
Everybody gets treated very badly on *24*! We did the running gag halfway through that I should be the one saying at the top of the show that this is the longest day of *my* life! So, my daughter goes missing, then she's kidnapped. I'm kidnapped myself, end up in this barn, then we're taken outside to be shot execution style. I have a cyst that bursts, which is very painful. I'm raped. I kill the guy who did that to me twice. My husband's been having an affair with Sarah Clarke. Then I forget everything – I think my daughter's died in a fiery car explosion and I get amnesia. Then I hook up with the guy that

I potentially had an affair with, but I can't remember him! Oh, and then I find out I'm pregnant!

As an actress, did you ever think: 'Surely this woman can suffer no more!'?

After years of playing parts that weren't as challenging, it was great fun. During the course of that year, I was challenged in ways I haven't done since I used to run a theatre company. Generally in television, particularly if you're a woman, and as you get older, you get relegated to the hero's wife, which I thought this was going to be initially. So firstly, I actually got to take a kick at that can and play all those possibilities for a woman, and secondly, I got to play them in a way that was true to myself and not in a typical television way. It was a huge, huge gift. And I will say, when the amnesia storyline came down the pipe, and after I got past the part of saying to the director 'I'm really nervous about this', and he says, 'Well, yes you should be', there was a bit of a relief about not having to carry 13 shows of drama behind me.

So you got to press the reset button?

Exactly. It was a 24-hour day in TV time, but for us it was eight, nine, ten months of shooting.

Is this a good time to be an actress in Hollywood?

I think it's been a good time for women in television for a while. Kiefer and I talked about this at the beginning of the show, that you sort of get to the point as an actor, and this is more specific to him coming from film, where you think, 'Why shouldn't I do television?' The writing, generally, consistently seems to be better and you're not actually responsible for carrying $80 million of revenue, and I think television has opened up possibilities for women that film has yet to catch up with. There's a huge gap right now in the States between those huge movies and the tiny independent ones. There doesn't seem to be a lot in between any more. Certainly when I was coming up, you could still make an Oliver Stone movie for $8 million, these little movies where actors like me who weren't big stars, had a chance. Those have largely gone away now.

How was the format of *24* sold to you before you signed up?
I auditioned and I didn't have a script, I had a scene. And the auditions went really well really fast, and I got in so quickly that I was getting embarrassed to ask for a script. All I knew was that I had a scene with this guy who I thought I was married to – I didn't know it was Kiefer, I didn't know the concept, I didn't know anything else apart from I was in a kitchen with a guy. I sensed, thankfully, it wasn't a comedy. When I found out what the show was about, I thought it was really smart and innovative, but I, probably like a lot of people, didn't know how they could sustain it for 24 episodes. But I think they did, and I really feel like those writers and that team of producers managed to keep the balls up in the air unfailingly for the entire season. It's a huge credit to them. There was a reality of trying to make five major storylines interconnect like a puzzle, and when we started we didn't know that we had the full 24, we were commissioned for 13 episodes originally.

You don't get to spend an awful lot of time with Jack in the series...
Traditionally on a show like this all the time we were on the phone, I'd go in for my day and say my lines into the phone, and have a continuity woman who would do the off camera lines. But we established in the pilot that we would all be there in the studio for each other's phone calls as if we were actually doing the scene. Part of it was because it's that much easier to edit the split screen, you need everything to be in synch. The other part of it, I think, particularly between Kiefer and I, we decided that when doing the pilot, if this was the connection we had to have and had to play our

relationship and make it understood, then we had to be there for each other in real life. So, although I didn't share screen time with Kiefer, we actually felt like we were working with each other a lot.

Did you get a lot of fan reaction to your character?
(Laughs) The first wave of it was a lot of Kiefer Sutherland fans saying 'She doesn't deserve him! I'm the girl for Kiefer!' There was that round. Then there was the rape scene, and there was a modicum of controversy in the States about, one: whether I do that, and two: that it couldn't possibly have happened, because the reaction that we filmed was for Teri not to fall into a blubbering mess but to keep going forwards to save our lives. Our director on that episode, Stephen Hopkins, is an Englishman, and he said 'It's just another day in the life at the BBC, we have rape stuff all the time, it's gritty and awful, and people just carry on!' (Laughs). When the rape thing happened, the fans were divided between mothers and women closer to my own age saying, 'That's exactly what I would have done,' and young men who couldn't imagine that anything sexual could happen to a mother! (Laughs). It was really hard for them to wrap their head around the fact that this wouldn't break the character.

If there were a *24* convention, would you consider attending?
Are you kidding? I love this show! I'm hugely proud of the show, I think it's great and I would do anything to support it being watched.

Interview conducted by Mark Wright in London, July 2002

Previously on 24

24 Season One [2001/2002]

'The following takes place on the day of the California presidential primary... Events occur in real time.'

12:00A.M. - 1:00A.M.

Written by **Robert Cochran and Joel Surnow**
Directed by **Stephen Hopkins**
CTU Special Agent in Charge Jack Bauer is assigned to protect Senator David Palmer from a predicted assassination attempt. Jack's daughter Kimberley has disappeared and his wife Teri has gone to search for her with a man she believes to be Alan York. Aboard a 747, a photographer on his way to meet Senator Palmer is seduced by a girl called Mandy. Shortly afterwards, the 747 is destroyed above the Mojave Desert...

1:00 A.M. – 2:00 A.M.

Written by Michael Loceff and Joel Surnow

Directed by Stephen Hopkins

Jack comes into a possession of a keycard belonging to a suspected mole within CTU. Teri continues to search for Kim, but is Alan York all he seems? Ira Gaines runs into problems retrieving the photographer's security pass from Mandy, and Kim gets into deeper trouble. Jamey Farrell traces the ownership of the CTU keycard to Nina Myers.

2:00 A.M. – 3:00 A.M.

Written by Michael Loceff and Joel Surnow

Directed by Stephen Hopkins

As Senator Palmer begins to learn that the death of his daughter's rapist seven years ago may be closer to home than he thought, Jack delivers the corrupt keycard to Jamey at CTU. Kim attempts to escape from her captors.

3:00 A.M. – 4:00 A.M.

Written by Robert Cochran

Directed by Winrich Kolbe

Jack investigates an address that Jamey managed to extract from data held on the keycard. District Director George Mason has CTU placed under lockdown, pending an investigation into the current situation. Alan York begins to show his true colours when he and Teri are pulled over for speeding. A suspect taken into custody by Jack tells him, 'If you ever want to see your daughter again, get me out of this!'

4:00A.M. - 5:00A.M.

Written by **Chip Johannsessen**

Directed by **Winrich Kolbe**

Palmer confronts his son Keith about the death of rapist Lyle Gibson and Jack goes against Mason's orders to break his suspect out of custody. Teri and Alan trace Janet, Kim's friend and Alan's daughter, to a local hospital, and Kim is delivered to Ira Gaines.

5:00A.M. - 6:00A.M.

Written by **Howard Gordon**

Directed by **Bryan Spicer**

Alan York reveals that that is exactly who he *isn't.* Kimberley helps to bury Rick's murdered partner-in-crime, and Jack and Teri are reunited at the hospital. Their reunion is brief, as Ira Gaines chooses to play his hand and begins his coercion of Jack.

6:00A.M. - 7:00A.M.

Written by **Andrea Newman**

Directed by **Bryan Spicer**

Teri discovers the truth about 'Alan York' to her cost, while Gaines orders Jack to switch the corrupt keycard with a decoy. Palmer prepares to make a difficult announcement to the press and Rick agrees to help Kimberley escape. Jack shoots Nina.

7:00 A.M. - 8:00 A.M.

Written by **Joel Surnow and Michael Loceff**
Directed by **Stephen Hopkins**

Back at CTU, an unharmed Nina and Tony Almeida discover the identity of the mole within the organisation. Teri is reunited with Kim when she arrives at Gaines's headquarters. Meanwhile Jack, still under the influence of Gaines, is arrested for the attempted assassination of Senator David Palmer.

8:00 A.M. - 9:00 A.M.

Written by **Virgil Williams**
Directed by **Stephen Hopkins**

Teri steps in to make a personal sacrifice to protect her daughter from their kidnappers, as Jack escapes custody and takes a waitress hostage. At CTU, Nina and Tony interrogate Jamey, and Sherry Palmer persuades a journalist not to go public with a story about her children.

9:00 A.M. - 10:00 A.M.

Written by **Lawrence Hertzog**
Directed by **Davis Guggenheim**

Gaines is unhappy to discover that his employers, the Drazens, have a back-up plan that does not involve him. Nina helps Jack to evade capture by the police and Jamey Farrell commits suicide. Teri and Kim are able to contact CTU.

10:00A.M. - 11:00A.M.

Written by Robert Cochran

Directed by Davis Guggenheim

As Teri begins to suffer from abdominal pains, Jack poses as a limo driver to intercept a possible suspect. Palmer begins to suspect that his wife may have her own agenda within his presidential campaign. The Drazens put their secondary plan into action and Jack sets out to find his family.

11:00A.M. - 12:00P.M.

Written by Howard Gordon

Directed by Stephen Hopkins

Acting Director Alberta Green interrogates Nina and Tony as to Jack's whereabouts while Jack gets closer to his family's location. Unknown to him, Teri and Kim are already making their own plans to escape. Jack has a reunion with his wife and daughter that almost ends in tragedy.

12:00P.M. - 1:00P.M.

Written by Andrea Newman

Directed by Stephen Hopkins

Palmer's relationship with Sherry continues to sour. Separated from Jack, Teri and Kim make their way to the rendezvous point while Jack and an injured Rick attempt to evade Gaines's men and catch up with them. After a game of cat and mouse, Jack kills Ira Gaines, and he and his family are choppered to safety. However, CTU learns that a second assassin has already arrived in Los Angeles.

1:00 P.M. - 2:00 P.M.

Written by **Joel Surnow and Michael Loceff**

Directed by **John Cassar**

Palmer is shocked to discover that planted evidence could implicate his son in a case of murder. Jack's debriefing begins and Teri and Kim are taken to a hospital for examination. Palmer arrives at CTU and demands to see Agent Bauer.

2:00 P.M. - 3:00 P.M.

Written by **Michael Chernuchin**

Directed by **John Cassar**

The connection between Bauer and Palmer is revealed – the Senator authorised a mission that Jack commanded two years previously. Teri and Kim have been transported to a CTU safe house where Nina will debrief them. At the safe house, Teri discovers she is pregnant. The assassin, identified as Alexis Drazen, has made a connection with one of Palmer's staff.

3:00 P.M. - 4:00 P.M.

Written by **Robert Cochran and Howard Gordon**

Directed by **Stephen Hopkins**

Drazen's men attack the safe house, but Teri and Kim manage to escape. Palmer discovers the relationship between staffer Elizabeth Nash and Alexis Drazen – Jack and Mason think they can use this to their advantage. Teri believes that Kim has died when their car explodes after falling over an embankment. The trauma causes Teri to suffer amnesia.

4:00 P.M. – 5:00 P.M.

Written by **Michael Chernuchin**

Directed by **Stephen Hopkins**

Jack supervises the operation to use Elizabeth Nash to plant a tracker on her lover, Alexis Drazen, but the plan ends in disaster when Nash stabs Alexis. Still stricken with amnesia, Teri finds herself at a familiar restaurant, and meets the man she nearly had an affair with – but can't remember him. Jack decides to pose as Alexis to get closer to the terrorists.

5:00 P.M. – 6:00 P.M.

Written by **Maurice Hurley**

Directed by **Fred Keller**

Kim gets into deeper trouble when she turns to Rick for help. Another CTU operation goes awry when the contact Jack makes is shot. Palmer plays his wife at her own game. Teri's friend, Parslow, takes her to the Bauer home, but they are being watched by Drazen operatives.

6:00 P.M. – 7:00 P.M.

Written by **Joel Surnow and Michel Loceff**

Directed by **Fred Keller**

Palmer goes public with his son's involvement in the death of his daughter's rapist. Teri comes face to face with Drazen's men once more, which jogs her memory, and Kim is desperate to escape her new situation. While exploring the deserted location given to them by Palmer, a chopper flies over Jack and Mason. Somebody knows they are there.

7:00P.M. – 8:00P.M.

Written by **Robert Cochran and Howard Gordon**
Directed by **Stephen Hopkins**

Jack is shocked to discover that Victor Drazen is still alive, incarcerated in a top secret detention centre that is about to come under attack from Drazen's son. The American public responds favourably to Palmer's press conference, and the Senator realises his marriage is over. Kim is arrested, while her father awaits the attack on the detention centre...

8:00P.M. – 9:00P.M.

Written by **Robert Cochran and Howard Gordon**
Directed by **Stephen Hopkins**

Jack is taken hostage by Victor Drazen and his son, Andre, just as Palmer sweeps to victory in the elections. Kim briefly experiences life on the inside and her mother is returned safely to CTU. As Kim is being transported to CTU by the police, a van smashes into the car, and masked men pull Kim from the wreck.

9:00P.M. – 10:00P.M.

Written by **Joel Surnow and Michael Loceff**
Directed by **Paul Shapiro**

Victor Drazen offers CTU a deal – Jack Bauer for his critically injured son Alexis, a trade which Mason declines. Palmer intercedes and orders Mason to agree to Drazen's demands. Teri is kept in the dark about the whereabouts of Kim, and Jack once again finds himself acting under duress from the Drazen family.

10:00 P.M. – 11:00 P.M.

Written by **Robert Cochran and Howard Gordon**

Directed by **Paul Shapiro**

The Drazens set a trap for Senator Palmer, once again using Jack as their unwilling tool. Palmer encourages rumours of his own death to help save Kim, and somebody close to Jack reveals herself to be a traitor.

11:00 P.M. – 12:00 A.M.

Teleplay by **Joel Surnow and Michael Loceff**

Story by **Robert Cochran and Howard Gordon**

Directed by **Stephen Hopkins**

The final chapter. Jack races against time to save both Kim and Teri, but he is too late, as Teri is brutally murdered at the hands of Nina Myers…

The Episodes

24

Season Two

(2002/2003)
24x45 minutes

An Imagine Television and
Twentieth Century Fox Television Production
In Association with Real Time Productions

Starring
Kiefer Sutherland as Jack Bauer
Sarah Wynter as Kate Warner
Elisha Cuthbert as Kimberley Bauer
Xander Berkeley as George Mason
Carlos Bernard as Tony Almeida
Penny Johnson Jerald as Sherry Palmer
And Dennis Haysbert as President David Palmer

Created by Joel Surnow and Robert Cochran
Executive Producers: Brian Grazer, Tony Krantz,
Howard Gordon, Robert Cochran, Joel Surnow
Co-Producers: Robin Chamberlin, Paul Gadd
Consulting Producer: Gil Grant
Producers: Kiefer Sutherland, Michael Loceff,
Jon Cassar, Cyrus Yavneh
Co-Executive Producer: Remi Aubuchon
Original Music: Sean Callery
Casting: Debi Manwiller, Peggy Kennedy
Director of Photography: Rodney Charters
Film Editing: Chris Willingham, David Latham
Production Design: Joseph Hodges
Costume Design: James Lapidus
Set Decoration: Cloudia Rebar
Special Effects Supervisor: Stan Blackwell
Written by: Joel Surnow, Robert Cochran, Remi Aubuchon,
Neil Cohen, Elizabeth M. Cosin, Duppy Demetrius,
David Ehrman, Gil Grant, Howard Gordon, Maurice Hurley,
Evan Katz, Michael Loceff, Virgil Williams

Production code: 2AFF01

Written by Joel Surnow and Michael Loceff
Directed by Jon Cassar

> *'The following takes place between 8:00A.M. and 9:00A.M.... Events occur in real time.'*

Guest Starring: Vicellous Shannon (Keith Palmer), Reiko Aylesworth (Michelle Dessler), Skye McCole Bartusiak (Megan Matheson), Billy Burke (Gary Matheson), Timothy Carhart (Eric Rayburn), Michelle Forbes (Lynne Kresge), Sara Gilbert (Paula Schaeffer), Laura Harris (Marie Warner), Tracy Middendorf (Carla Matheson), Phillip Rhys (Reza Naiyeer), John Terry (Bob Warner), Tamlyn Tomita (Jenny Dodge), Jim Abele (Ralph Burton), Mike Saad (Prime Minister), Esther K. Chae (Mina), Billy Mayo (Agent Rosser), Tony Lee (Deng), R.A. Buck (Colonel Graham)

FIELD REPORT

08:00A.M. – SEOUL, SOUTH KOREA. A man is being brutally tortured for information, which he eventually gives up. One of his torturers runs to another room where four men sit around a table. Waiting. 'When?' asks one of them. 'Today.' One of the men picks up a phone and asks to speak to Eric Rayburn, NSA. **08:02A.M.** President David Palmer is enjoying a vacation with his son, Keith, fishing on Lake Oswego in Oregon. Palmer asks Keith how his mother is, but is interrupted by his bodyguard. There is a situation… In Los Angeles, Kim Bauer has been working as an au pair for Gary and Carla Matheson, looking after their daughter, Megan. Kim is getting dressed, and helps Megan play a game of hide and seek with her father – a nice moment of domestic happiness.

Palmer's morning of fishing is cut short at the request of the National Security Agency (NSA). Palmer apologises to Keith and consults with his press secretary, Jenny Dodge. He asks her how bad the situation is, and she replies that it must be bad – to her knowledge, no President has ever been re-routed on a morning off. **08:06A.M.** At CTU in Los Angeles, Paula Schaeffer consults with Tony Almeida on a point of procedure, which he readily admits he couldn't care less about. Tony advises George Mason about a meeting he is setting up with LAX airport to discuss security upgrades, and Mason replies with his usual dismissive manner, complaining that he should be in Washington by now (a reference to Palmer's deal with Mason in Day One: 09:00P.M. – 10:00P.M.). Michelle Dessler gives Mason a message from Eric Rayburn of the NSA, who wants Mason to take care of a special request. Mason thinks there must be some mistake and heads to his office. Michelle tells Tony that they've been asked to bring in Jack Bauer.

Palmer arrives at the Northwest Regional Operations facility, where he is met by Eric Rayburn, who informs the President that they have a very serious domestic terrorist situation on their hands.

Rayburn briefs Palmer fully – a nuclear device is hidden somewhere in Los Angeles and is expected to go off in the next 24 hours. A group known as Second Wave are believed to be responsible, a group with unofficial links to an unnamed Middle Eastern state.

08:12A.M. Kimberley has breakfast with the Mathesons. After Carla leaves, Gary tells Kim she has a great body, which makes her uncomfortable. Palmer speaks to the Prime Minister of the Middle Eastern state. He informs the Prime Minister that the US is aware of his country's affiliation to Second Wave. This is denied. Palmer makes it clear to the politician that if a bomb goes off on US soil today, it will only hurt America, but will destroy the Prime Minister's country. A bearded Jack Bauer watches Kim from his car as she plays with Megan. His phone rings, but Jack refuses to take the call as it's from George Mason and he doesn't work for CTU any more. Kim hasn't really spoken to her father since Teri's death and isn't exactly pleased to see him. She is missing him but not ready to see him yet, as the memories of her mother's death are still painful. Jack leaves with nothing resolved between Kim and himself.

08:17A.M. Palmer summons Rayburn to his office to ask why a casualty assessment has not yet been made. Rayburn assures him that the figures are being prepared, and tells the President that it's time he had a 'serious' conversation with the Pentagon. Palmer tells him that they don't know who to retaliate against. They are both aware that the Prime Minister was lying about his country's affiliation to Second Wave, but the Prime Minister may not be responsible for the current situation. Palmer's priority at this stage is to protect American lives.

08:22A.M. On the morning of his wedding, Reza Naiyeer arrives at the Warner residence, home of his wife-to-be, Marie. Preparations for the wedding are underway. Marie's sister, Kate, tells her father, Bob Warner, that she's unhappy he let Reza send the company car to pick up his cousin. Warner is amazed that his daughter isn't able to trust Reza yet and asks her if it's because he's

from the Middle East. Kate tells him not be ridiculous, but there's something she doesn't trust.

At CTU, Mason receives a call from Rayburn, asking on their progress in locating Jack Bauer. Mason warns against bringing in Bauer due to his current condition, but Rayburn is insistent and Mason says there's only one thing that will persuade Bauer to come back to CTU.

08:24 A.M. Jack arrives home to a ringing phone. Tony leaves a message for Jack to call him urgently, which is ignored. He opens a drawer and almost picks up a gun, but instead retrieves a family picture of himself with Teri and Kim. As he curls up on the sofa clutching the picture, the phone rings again. It is the President, and Jack answers. Palmer tells Jack he is needed, to which Jack replies that he's inactive and not sure in his current condition how he could help. Palmer appreciates this is still a difficult time, but begs him to go to CTU and listen to what they have to say.

08:28 A.M. Kim is surprised when Carla returns home. She is wrapping a gift for Gary's assistant, which Kim offers to finish. Carla nervously tells Kim that her husband likes things done a specific way, then asks her to take Megan upstairs. At CTU, Michelle alerts Tony to an Information Flow Advisory – something big is happening and it's going to be inter-agency. Tony asks her to start filtering data coming into CTU. Paula enthusiastically offers to help, and Michelle tells her to stop trying too hard and just do her job.

08:31 A.M. Mason addresses all CTU department heads with a priority announcement. He has just come off a conference call with the NSA and Division, and he informs the team that there is a nuclear device in Los Angeles, set to go off during the day. From this point on, there is to be no communication outside CTU's secured envelope – in other words, nobody is to call home. It's time to do their jobs. Tony tells Mason that he hasn't yet reached Jack Bauer.

Palmer receives further briefing from Rayburn on the expected casualties if the device were to go off. The worst case scenario points towards somewhere in the region of two and a half million casualties and global repercussions for years. Rayburn urges the President to speak to the Joint Chiefs of Staff, but Palmer is adamant this is not yet a military operation.

08:36A.M. An unidentified man enters a factory building where a bomb is being constructed. He asks when the bomb will be ready. 'Soon,' his associate tells him. At CTU, Paula has a crisis of confidence about whether she can operate under this kind of pressure. Tony assures her she can. As Paula heads off to work, Jack Bauer arrives at CTU. Tony immediately shows him to the conference room for a briefing with Mason, Michelle and Paula. Jack gets straight to the point and asks what he's doing at CTU. On hearing about the bomb, Jack calls Kim to tell her that they have to leave LA together, today. Kim doesn't listen and hangs up. Jack is all for hotfooting it out of CTU (and who can blame him?), and Tony tries to talk him round, but fails. Out in the car park, Jack has a change of heart and agrees to help, on condition that Kim is taken to safety, and he liaises with Tony – *only* Tony. He doesn't trust Mason or anybody else. Jack is fully briefed. The prime suspect they are after is Joseph Wald, who has links to Second Wave. Jack was called in because he was previously involved in an undercover operation with Wald. Jack put him behind bars. Wald is out on appeal awaiting a new trial, but is not at any of his registered addresses. The key witness in the trial is one Marshall Goren. Jack asks for him to be brought in.

08:46A.M. Kate receives a phone call from Ralph Burton, a private detective she hired to run a check on her future brother-in-law. Reza had previously checked out, but his name has now come up in connection with another case, connecting him to known terrorist Syed Ali. Burton tells Kate he will need her help to establish if Reza's link to Ali is legitimate or if he is, in fact, a terrorist.

08:49A.M. Palmer is angry when Rayburn attempts to set up a conference with the Joint Chiefs behind his back. At CTU, Michelle assists in setting up a fake background for Jack to go undercover once again. Mason asks Jack what his plan is, but he refuses to co-operate, barely acknowledging Mason's presence. Mason tells Jack that he looks like a bum off the street, and if he's about to lose it, Mason needs to know, because he hasn't got time to clean up one of Jack's messes again. Jack assures the CTU boss that he isn't losing it, as Marshall Goren is brought into the room. Michelle is dismissed, leaving Jack and Mason to interrogate their witness, and Jack takes a new approach to the art of questioning by pulling a gun and shooting Goren, much to Mason's horror. He asks for a hacksaw, along with a helicopter and a back-up team.

Kim and Megan are playing upstairs when Gary arrives home and gets into a violent argument with Carla. Megan tells Kim she doesn't like it when it gets like this. Kim locks the door when Gary comes upstairs, pretending she was washing Megan's hair. Gary asks if they heard anything and tries to send Kim out of the room. When she refuses, he turns violent and throws her to the floor. When Megan tries to run, Gary grabs her, but she falls and hits her head.

At CTU, Jack avails himself of the washroom facilities, shaving off his beard. He looks at himself in the mirror. Jack's back! Tick, tick, tick…

CTU INCIDENT REPORT

Haven't I Seen You Somewhere Before?: Reiko Aylesworth (Michelle Dessler) paid her dues on the daytime soap circuit, playing Rebecca Lewis in *One Life to Live*. She graduated to TV and film guest-starring roles, with appearances on TV in *The West Wing* and *Law and Order: Special Victims Unit*. Her film credits include *You've Got Mail* (1998), *Random Hearts* (1999) and *Man On The Moon* (1999). Vicellous Shannon (Keith Palmer) appeared in the TV series *Dangerous Minds* and has clocked up film roles in *Can't Hardly Wait* (1998), *The Hurricane* (1999) and

Hart's War (2002) alongside Bruce Willis and Colin Farrell. Skye McCole Bartusiak (Megan Matheson) played a young Marilyn Monroe in the mini-series *Blonde*, and her TV father Billy Burke (Gary Matheson) appeared opposite Michelle Forbes (Lynne Kresge) in the short-lived *Wonderland*. Tracy Middendorf (Carla Matheson) appeared in the recent TV revival of *The Time Tunnel* and played Laura Kingman in *Beverley Hills 90210*. Tamlyn Tomita (Jenny Dodge) played first officer Laurel Takashima in the pilot movie of *Babylon 5*, and voiced a character in the computer game *James Bond, 007: Nightfire*. She also has a recurring role in the popular *JAG* and appeared in the first season of *The Burning Zone*.

Behind The Camera: Co-writer Michael Loceff also serves as a producer on *24*. Before coming to *24* during its first season, Loceff had previously worked with Joel Surnow and Robert Cochran on *La Femme Nikita*, rendering his services as writer and story editor. He is also a professor at Foothills College, in Los Altos Hills, California. Director Jon Cassar began his TV directing career in the early 1990s, helming episodes of the Canadian vampire/detective series *Forever Night*. Since then he has directed episodes of *Due South*, *Baywatch Nights*, *Profiler* and *Mutant X*. Before becoming a producer/director on *24*, Cassar directed episodes of *La Femme Nikita*, coming into professional contact with *24* creators Joel Surnow and Robert Cochran.

Time Checks: Rayburn tells the president that Park broke his silence on the bomb about **15 minutes** ago. This indicates that the torture session must have been in progress several minutes before the opening of the episode. Kate tells Reza he's not due to marry her sister for another **ten hours**. Palmer tells Jack that he's been thinking about him a lot over the past **year**. Jack has been inactive for **over a year**. Michelle asks Tony if he's looked at his system in the last **five minutes**. A properly configured nuclear warhead would irradiate 100 square miles in **seconds**. Jack says it will take him **six weeks** to re-establish undercover connections with Wald, and Mason wants him to do it in **two hours**.

Fashion Police: Kim's skimpy shorts score a home run off the first ball. Elisha Cuthbert looks like she's been on the low carb diet all summer, and the producers have been paying attention to all those *FHM* covers. Palmer's shirt is a big giveaway that there's been no woman in his life since he kicked Sherry out of the White House – salmon pink? Really, David! Thankfully, in the intervening year Tony has had time to go home and shave off his annoying tufty soul patch, but that would appear to be all. You could have changed your suit too, mate. Finally, Jack does himself no favours with this year's look from the Hicks R Us ensemble collection. We know you're still hurting from losing the missus, but plaid shirts and bum fluff are not the way forward, trust us.

The Perils Of Kim: And she was doing so well, bless her. After a great start in the skimpy shorts department and displaying that she has natural skill as a nanny, Kim chooses to ignore her father's really rather sensible suggestion that they get out of Los Angeles, playing the 'I'm not ready' card for the second time this week. Some would say it's a natural reaction considering what happened to her mother last time she had any involvement with CTU. But honestly, putting her phone straight to voicemail is just downright childish.

It's Not Easy Being Jack: Jack has a painful sense of ennui about his person throughout most of this hour, with Kim not helping much, it must be said. He spends most of the episode looking lost and about to burst into tears. How could anybody not want to give him a hug and mother the poor love? Things perk up a bit when he arrives at CTU amid much whispering and promptly proceeds to shoot Marshall Goren. Obviously pumping George Mason with a tranq dart in **Day One**: **12:00 – 01:00 A.M** wasn't enough, and his request for a hacksaw is persuading no one that he's got a full six-pack in the cool box. Thank goodness he shaves off the beard by the end, making it very clear that Jack Bauer is well and truly back. You go boy!

Great Lines:

Mason: 'Tony, tell you what, if I'm still here this time next year, take me out to the woodshed and shoot me.'

Jack: 'That's the problem with people like you, George. You want results, but you never want to get your hands dirty. I'd start rolling up your sleeves. I'm gonna need a hacksaw.'

Death Count: The rather unfortunate Marshall Goren getting offed by Jack brings up our death count to a measly one. But it's early days yet.

Trivia: OK, how's this for obscure TV show connections? Tamlyn Tomita played Laurel Takashima in the pilot episode of *Babylon 5*, although she would not become a regular cast member. Bruce Boxleitner took over the lead in *Babylon 5* from the second season onwards, and he is married to actress Melissa Gilbert, who is best known as buck-toothed Laura Ingles in *Little House on the Prairie*. Melissa Gilbert is the sister of Sara Gilbert, who plays Paula Schaeffer in *24*. Phew! Glad we got that cleared up.

DEBRIEF

On 29 October 2002, *24* was back on the Fox network. As first episodes go, this is absolutely fine. There are 23 more episodes ahead, so there's plenty of time for the usual twisty-turniness, and this has just the right pace to reacquaint ourselves with old faces and get to know the new guys. The best standout moment that tells us we're dealing with a whole new Jack Bauer is the request for a hacksaw. Perfect!

Thanks to some lucrative sponsorship by Ford, the first episode was transmitted without commercial breaks. The episode ran approximately eight minutes longer than a standard episode, with the remainder of the hour taken up by extended Ford advertising and trails for upcoming Fox programming. It's a sure sign of the success and high profile that *24* gained with a certain demographic that led to this fanfared opening, and it worked.

For the repeat showing on Fox dated 4 November 2002, the episode was shown standard length, with around eight minutes of footage deleted. This deleted footage may end up on the expected DVD release for the series, but it is unlikely that this material will ever be shown on US TV again. For the completists out there, the following is a rundown of the excised footage:

1) Palmer apologises to Keith and consults with his press secretary, Jenny Dodge. He asks her how bad the situation is, and she replies that it must be bad – to her knowledge, no President has ever been re-routed on a morning off. (46 seconds approx.)

2) Kimberley has breakfast with the Mathesons. After Carla leaves, Gary tells Kim she has a great body, which makes her uncomfortable. (1 minute, 31 seconds approx.)

3) Mason receives a call from Rayburn, asking on their progress in locating Jack Bauer. Mason warns against bringing Bauer in due to his current condition, but Rayburn is insistent and Mason says there's only one thing that will persuade Bauer to come back to CTU. (40 seconds approx.)

4) Michelle alerts Tony to the Information Flow Advisory. Mason addresses all CTU department heads with an announcement about the bomb. Tony tells Mason that he hasn't yet reached Jack Bauer. (2 minutes, 32 seconds approx.)

5) Paula has a crisis of confidence about whether she can operate under this kind of pressure. Tony assures her she can. (1 minute, 15 seconds approx.)

6) Palmer is angry when Rayburn attempts to set up a conference with the Joint Chiefs behind his back. (1 minute, 24 seconds approx.)

Pulse Rate: 100 bpm (but plus five for a few seconds when Jack shoots Marshall Goren)

Questions Arising:

- Why has Palmer not made good on his promise to promote Mason to a position in Washington within one month of taking office?
- Why is Rayburn so eager for Palmer to put the operation in the hands of the military?
- Is Teri Bauer really dead?
- What connection does Reza have to Syed Ali?

9:00 A.M.

10:00 A.M.

Production Code 2AFF02

Written by Joel Surnow and Michael Loceff
Directed by Jon Cassar

> *'The following takes place between 9:00A.M. and 10:00A.M.... Events occur in real time.'*

Guest Starring: Reiko Aylesworth (Michelle Dessler), Skye McCole Bartusiak (Megan Matheson), Billy Burke (Gary Matheson), Timothy Carhart (Eric Rayburn), Michelle Forbes (Lynne Kresge), Sara Gilbert (Paula Schaeffer), Laura Harris (Marie Warner), Tracy Middendorf (Carla Matheson), Phillip Rhys (Reza Naiyeer), Tamlyn Tomita (Jenny Dodge), Douglas O'Keeffe (Eddie Grant), Jimmi Simpson (Chris), Gregory Sporleder (Dave), Michael Holden (Ron Wieland), Jim Abele (Ralph Burton), Terry Bozeman (Richard Armus), Alicia Bien (Reporter)

FIELD REPORT

09:00A.M. Lynne Kresge briefs Palmer on the CIA's proposed response to the nuclear threat. Palmer is keen to avoid mass hysteria amongst the public – under no circumstances must the story be leaked. At the factory building, the bomb is loaded on to a delivery truck by a group of unnamed men and driven out on to the streets of Los Angeles. Gary finishes his call in Kim's bathroom, and the two girls make a run for it. Downstairs, Carla gives Kim the keys to her car and tells her to take Megan. Gary runs after them as they get in the car, telling Kim he will kill her if she does this. Kim drives off as Gary phones his security company and asks for the location of the car to be tracked.

09:04A.M. En route by chopper to a drop-off point to pick up a car, Michelle briefs Jack on the known members of Joseph Wald's crew. He recognises Eddie Grant, one of Wald's main associates with whom Jack was friends while undercover. Jack asks Michelle if they have any more intelligence on the size of the bomb. She tells him that they don't. Lynne tells Palmer that they've started getting questions from the press as to why the President cut short his fishing trip. He says he'll take care of it, but Rayburn tells him they have a lot to get through and this is no time to coddle the media. Palmer replies that he wants to avoid any rumours. As the chopper touches down, Jack calls Tony, but Mason answers. Jack asks if they've got to Kim yet, and he is told that Kim wasn't at the house. Mason assures Jack that they'll take care of Kim. Jack tries calling Kim's mobile, but she left it at the Mathesons'. He leaves a message on her voicemail, once again urging her to get out of LA. At CTU, Tony assures a frightened Paula that the nuclear bomb may only be a false alarm. Mason learns that forged Middle Eastern passports found in a car that was crossing the border matched those of the suspects, and he sends the closest agent to investigate – the agent assigned to pick up Kim.

09:09A.M. Jack arrives at the salvage garage being used as a base by Wald's gang. He is met by Eddie Grant who knows Bauer as Jack Roush. He accuses Jack of putting Wald in jail, but Jack tries to square himself by saying that he has news about Marshall Goren turning state's evidence to convict Wald. He gives Eddie the present he's carrying in his bag – the decapitated head of Marshall Goren. Eddie smiles, seemingly convinced by this macabre tribute, and brings Jack into the back room.

09:16A.M. Palmer holds an informal press conference to put the media off the scent. Jenny informs him that a journalist, Ron Wieland, is suspicious that something is going on. Palmer tells Jenny to keep an eye on him.

09:17A.M. Kim drives Megan to the nearest police station, but they hit traffic on the way. Megan is complaining about head pains, and Kim decides to take a short cut down an alley, just as Gary drives up to block their path. Kim attempts to reverse, but the alley is blocked by a van, and as Gary approaches, the two girls make a run for it once again with Gary in pursuit. As the girls hide, Gary pleads for Megan to call out, saying that Kim is going to hurt her. When she doesn't respond he becomes angry.

09:20A.M. Grant introduces Jack to the rest of the group, who are immediately suspicious. Jack says all he wants is to talk to Joe, and then he'll be gone. One of the gang, Dave, insists on checking Jack's records and goes online. At CTU, everyone is taken by surprise that the gang is checking Jack's records so soon. They haven't yet planted the fake data. Paula improvises as Michelle and Tony race to get the final data in place. When the data fails to come up on screen, Grant pulls his gun, ready to kill Jack, but Paula finally makes the file transfers and everything checks out. Jack is in.

09:28A.M. Never knowing when to give up, Rayburn once again attempts to persuade Palmer to have a meeting with the Pentagon. Palmer, ever consistent, tells him to go away. Lynne comes to Palmer's office with news about Ron Wieland. He has persuaded his network to let him go live with an exclusive that the country's alert condition has changed and that Palmer is managing a situation. Palmer asks Lynne to set up a private interview with Wieland and to bring in Armus.

09:31 A.M. Jack watches Dave working with explosives, and is baiting him when Eddie walks back in. He tells him to come back tomorrow as they have something going down. Jack says goodbye and gets into his car to call Mason. Mason tells him that Wald's threat rating has just been upped and they need to get to him, so Jack is to stick with Grant's crew. As a van pulls up with the rest of the crew and they prepare to leave, Jack fakes engine problems and opens up the bonnet.

09:33 A.M. Mason checks a confidential report from Division that gives the probability of the bomb detonating. On reading this, he packs his briefcase and heads downstairs. He tells Tony that he's got to follow up a lead in Bakersfield. Tony challenges him, saying he's trying to get outside the blast radius. Mason tells him to mind his own business and leaves the building.

09:40 A.M. While she and Kimberly are hiding in an alley, Megan complains that her head hurts. Kim hides her behind some boxes and tells her to wait while she goes to make a phone call.

09:42 A.M. Kate calls Ralph Burton to tell him she's been unable to find Reza's wallet. He asks her to look for Reza's passport instead so they can find out which countries he's been to in the last six months. While Reza deals with wedding arrangements, Kate finds the passport amongst his belongings in his car. She writes down the information, just before Reza finds her sitting in the car. She tells him she needed to move the car to make space for other vehicles.

09:45 A.M. As Jack tends to the car, Dave comes over to tell him to get lost. Jack tells him to mind his own business, and shouts over to Grant that Dave had packed the fuses too tight. Dave lunges at Jack, and, in true Bauer style, Jack breaks his ankle.

09:50 A.M. Kim finds a pay phone and calls 911, but Gary surprises her. He is strangely reasonable, saying he didn't mean to hurt his wife and only wants to apologise to Megan. Kim doesn't believe him and he gets forceful, causing Kim to take a leaf out of her dad's book and knee him in the groin. Gary comes after her, obviously not getting the message, and Kim smashes his face with a tyre iron.

Kate calls Burton, to give him the information. The private detective will cross-check Reza's movements against those of Syed Ali to see if there is a connection. Marie interrupts the call to thank her sister for all the help she's given with the wedding. They hug.

09:54 A.M. Palmer meets with Ron Wieland. Wieland says he knows that the alert condition has been changed and his story is ready to go. Palmer tells him he is wrong, but Wieland, knowing how difficult it is to get a meeting with the President that quickly, thinks otherwise. Palmer asks him to hold off on the story, and he'll give him a head start on a briefing set for tomorrow. Wieland says he'll think about it and leaves. Palmer calls Armus. As Wieland leaves the residence, Secret Service Agent Richard Armus introduces himself, telling the journalist there's something the President wants him to see. Wieland is led away.

09:57 A.M. With Dave's ankle broken, Grant asks Jack to take the man's place on the crew. Kim returns from her fight with Gary to find Megan, but the girl is gone. Jack rides in the van with Eddie Grant and his crew. He asks Grant what the job is. He replies that they're going to blow up CTU. Tick, tick, tick...

CTU INCIDENT REPORT

Haven't I Seen You Somewhere Before?: Michelle Forbes (Lynne Kresge) made her TV debut in the long-running American soap *The Guiding Light*, but is perhaps best known as the surly, insubordinate Ensign Ro Laren in *Star Trek: The Next Generation*. Forbes passed on the opportunity to be a lead in *Star Trek: Deep Space Nine*, choosing to pursue a movie career. In 1993 she was terrorised by Brad Pitt in *Kalifornia*, playing the girlfriend of David Duchovny. She also appeared in *Swimming With Sharks* (1994) and the appropriately titled *Escape From L.A.* (1996). Prior to *24*, Forbes was a regular on *Homicide: Life on the Street* for two years, played Ken Stott's wife in the BBC production *Messiah* and its sequel, and appeared opposite Billy Burke in the short-lived *Wonderland*. Douglas O'Keeffe (Eddie Grant) played Bruno Anselmo in *Dark Angel* and had a recurring role in *La Femme Nikita*. Gregory Sporleder (Dave) has had movie roles in *Black Hawk Down* (2001), *Being John Malkovich* (1999) and *The Rock* (1996).

Time Checks: Palmer tells Jenny he only found out about the bomb less than **an hour** ago. Dave thinks he can 'bird dog' Jack's records in **two minutes**. Ron Wieland will be going live on network TV for **ten minutes**, starting at noon. Grant tells somebody on the phone that he'll speak to them in **an hour** – does that indicate the job will be over by the end of the next episode? My cliffhanger sense is tingling!

Fashion Police: Blimey, Jack goes from Hicksville to The Blue Oyster Bar in a single bound. His shave last week must have gone to his head as he's now sporting a green bomber jacket and tight T-shirt, making him look like a regular cruiser down at Mardi Gras rather than a secret agent. Matters aren't helped by Grant's crew looking like they're the B-team for the Village People – sometimes, denim just isn't macho. And don't the Barbie Twins, Kate and Marie, look so dinky in their *Sunset Beach* shirts and slacks?

The Perils Of Kim: Kim starts off the episode with a heroic dash from the Matheson residence, but her luck couldn't last, could it? On her way to the police station, just as the traffic is starting to move forward again, she decides to take a short cut down an alley, straight into Gary's waiting arms. Wrong! Having said that, the lass proves she's a chip off the old Bauer block when she opens a can of whupass on the slimy Gary Matheson. But then she's coloured surprised when Megan does a runner at the end of the episode.

It's Not Easy Being Jack: Jack's general sense of rabid ennui has gone along with the beard. Maybe shooting Marshall Goren last week has made him remember that being a secret agent is cool – you get to jump out of helicopters and stuff. Poor old Dave should have known better than to mess with our Jack, and that decisive crack of ankle bone shows that he hasn't just been down the local dive drinking beer with the other bums for 18 months.

Great Lines:
Grant: 'You broke his damn ankle, Jack.'
Jack: 'He shouldn't have been playing with adults.'

Death Count: Surprisingly no one buys it big this week, although with Jack on his way to CTU with a bag full of plastique, you can bet that situation will be rectified by 11:00 A.M.

Trivia: Mason's laptop shows that the probability of the bomb's detonation is between 89–93 per cent. Mason (again) says he's heading to Bakersfield, which is approximately 58 miles from Los Angeles.

DEBRIEF

There's a nuclear bomb somewhere in LA, Jack is back in the field, Kim is on the run from a psychotic father, Palmer is getting gyp from the press, Tony is staring over computer monitors at the new chick and Mason is in a bad mood. There are no real surprises here, but the action and tension are upped a few degrees with Jack showing he still has balls with his skilful infiltration of Grant's team, and the head in a duffel bag moment is priceless. The players are all lining up on the pitch, so we may as well let the games begin!

In the background to the episode is much technical talk of bombs, and Eric Rayburn briefs the President and Lynne on the expected casualties from the detonation of a dirty bomb or nuclear device in Los Angeles. The jargon and technical terms being used assume a level of understanding on the part of the audience that may not have been present 12 months ago. In light of the terrible events of 11 September 2001, the use of terms like 'dirty bomb' and the now mantra-like 'weapons of mass destruction' are becoming commonplace across the media. But what is the reality behind those terms?

A dirty bomb is not much more powerful than a conventional explosive. It may also be referred to as a 'radiological weapon', and the difference between this and a standard bomb is the inclusion of radioactive material. It can be a dynamite-packed explosive, causing major damage on the initial detonation, and then further damage by airborne radiation contamination. Hence the expression 'dirty'.

Worryingly, the expertise required in putting together a dirty bomb requires no more knowledge than a conventional explosive. The difficulty comes in acquiring the radioactive material, so unless your Uncle Dave has a supply of Strontium 90 or Cesium 137 stashed away in the garden shed, forget it.

You'll be pleased to hear that no terrorist group has ever detonated a dirty bomb. In May 2002, an alleged al-Qaeda terrorist was arrested for making plans to construct such a device. Prior to this, a United Nations report indicated that Iraq conducted tests into the use of a one ton radiological weapon, but abandoned further tests as the radiation levels achieved were not deadly enough.

Anyone who wants to look up more information on dirty bombs (but, thankfully, not how to make them) can go to:

http:www.terrorismanswers.com/home/.

(Our normal, fun-filled trivia service will resume shortly.)

Pulse Rate: 103 bpm

Questions Arising:

- ? Where is Wieland getting his information?
- ? What fate awaits Ron Wieland?
- ? Where is Megan?
- ? Just what connection do the Barbie Twins and the wedding have to the bomb?

10:00 A.M. – 11:00 A.M.

Production Code 2AFF03

Written by Howard Gordon
Directed by James Whitmore Jr

> ***'The following takes place between 10:00A.M. and 11:00A.M.... Events occur in real time.'***

Guest Starring: Reiko Aylesworth (Michelle Dessler), Skye McCole Bartusiak (Megan Matheson), Billy Burke (Gary Matheson), Timothy Carhart (Eric Rayburn), Michelle Forbes (Lynne Kresge), Sara Gilbert (Paula Schaeffer), Laura Harris (Marie Warner), Phillip Rhys (Reza Naiyeer), John Terry (Bob Warner), Tamlyn Tomita (Jenny Dodge), Sal Landi (Sgt Arroyo), Scott Allan Campbell (Hazmat Doctor Porter), Antonio David Lyons (Cam Strocker), Douglas O'Keeffe (Eddie Grant), Jimmi Simpson (Chris), Jim Abele (Ralph Burton), Maurice G. Smith (CTU Security Guard), Ben Koldyke (Officer), Addie Daddio (O.C. Operator)

FIELD REPORT

10:00A.M. As Kim frantically searches for the missing Megan, Gary gives the police the name and description of the girl who he says kidnapped his daughter. As Mason, streak of yellow visibly showing, drives out of Los Angeles towards Bakersfield, Tony phones him with news that a suspect has been located in Panorama City. District has requested that Mason checks it out, and after some cajoling from Tony, he agrees.

At the Northwest Operations Centre, Lynne provides Palmer with updated casualty predictions. They are higher than anticipated. The possibility of a dirty bomb has been ruled out and the NSA now believes they are looking for a nuclear warhead. Kim finds Megan in the company of two unsavoury looking youths – the little one was scared and went looking for her au pair. Jack questions Eddie Grant about why CTU is being targeted, but Eddie isn't saying anything – he tells Jack to keep his eyes open, and the crew will do the rest. Jack's mobile rings – it is Kim. Jack can't talk, and tells her to check her phone messages. She tells her father what happened and asks him to come and get her. He tells her he can't and that she should go to Carol's. Jack hangs up on her, leaving Kim no choice but to call Tony at CTU. Tony tells her to get to CTU, just as the phone lines at CTU start to go down.

10:08A.M. CTU's phones have gone down thanks to the intervention of Grant at a relay station. He tells Jack that they're creating interference so a phone crew will be called to the building. Uncomfortable with Jack hanging around, Grant tells him to watch the road, giving Jack the opportunity to call CTU with a warning. He cannot get through, so instead dials another number and asks to speak to the President. The Operations Centre puts Jack through to Lynne Kresge as Palmer is speaking to the press corps. He gives her the urgent message that CTU must be evacuated as a bomb is going to be planted there. Jack has to cut short the call when Grant interrupts him.

10:09 A.M. Lynne informs Eric Rayburn of the upcoming hit on CTU. Rayburn presumes that this is a diversion from the main nuclear attack, and stops Lynne from informing the President and warning CTU. He believes it will blow Jack's cover and jeopardise his current mission to find Joseph Wald. Lynne says she doesn't work for him, and contacts Jenny Dodge to interrupt the press conference. At the relay station, a two-man crew arrives to tend to the problem, and Grant despatches one of the men with a silenced pistol. He orders the other man, Cam, to contact his boss to request an on-site systems check at CTU. Jack can only watch.

10:16 A.M. Tony receives a call from Rayburn asking for all of CTU's data relevant to the current threat to be transferred to the NSA server. Tony tells him it can't be done quickly and Rayburn snottily tells Tony to get started. Tony pulls Paula off her current task to take care of Rayburn's request. Michelle points out to Tony that if Rayburn's order was only precautionary, then other agencies would have received the same instructions. Tony asks her to look into this. Mason arrives at an industrial complex in Panorama City, where he meets with LAPD officers who matched a vehicle to the alert put out by CTU that morning. They haven't checked inside the building yet as they were waiting for Mason. An armed Mason accompanies the police into the building, where they find the equipment that was used to construct the bomb. As they investigate further a gunman fires out of the shadows and Mason and the officers shoot it out. An officer goes down, just as a glass panel shatters, dispersing green powder into the air. Another officer drops the gunman, and Mason, seeing the radioactive warning signs, screams for the officer to get out of the building as they have a hot zone.

10:21 A.M. Kim and Megan ride the bus to CTU. Megan asks if Kim's mother cries a lot, and Kim tells her that she doesn't have a mother, she passed away. Kim assures Megan that she is not the cause of Gary's anger, and promises that she will never let him hurt Megan again.

10:23A.M. The telephone repair team pulls up to CTU, and Cam lies to the security guard that he is there to fix the phones. Jack, Grant and the crew are in the back, and the guard, in true CTU tight security fashion, clears them into the car park. Cam asks what they could possibly want from CTU and Grant tells him they are taking back their country. 'We're patriots,' Jack tells him.

10:30A.M. Meanwhile, over in the *Sunset Beach* wedding subplot, Kate gets a call from Ralph Burton. He confirms that Reza has had contact with Syed Ali. Burton has now dobbed Kate's future brother-in-law in to the cops. Kate says she has to tell her sister that she is about to get married to a possible terrorist, but Burton tells her to sit tight. When she hangs up, Marie and Reza playfully try to coax her into meeting Reza's cousin, but Kate freaks out and runs to her room. Cue daytime-soap moment as Marie confronts her sister to ask what's wrong. Kate tells her she's just upset that she's about to lose her little sister. (Please, can somebody ask them to stop crying? This is *24*, not *Oprah*.) Lynne confronts Jenny about why she hasn't seen the President yet. The Press Secretary tells her that Palmer is still on camera and that she slipped him a note. She hurries off, leaving Rayburn to glance furtively at Lynne and twirl his moustache.

10:34A.M. As Eddie and his crew make their way into CTU, Jack waits in the van with the tied-up worker. He starts sketching a map showing the location of the bombs.

10:41A.M. As he and the police officers are being put through decontamination, Mason calls Tony to tell him about the lab. He tells Tony that they have three dead bodies and he's sending fingerprints through to see if they match any of the suspects. Tony informs him of Rayburn's order to transfer CTU's database to the NSA server. Mason tells him to contact Ryan Chappelle at Division to see what he can find out. The Hazmat officers ask Mason to strip off all his clothes and they begin to hose him down.

10:43A.M. Michelle approaches Paula in the restroom to ask if she has transferred the data to the NSA. She tells her superior that it's in process. Michelle assures Paula, who is worried about her family and friends living in LA, that everything will be OK.

As Grant's crew proceeds to secret the bombs around CTU (complete with not at all inconspicuous blue neon countdown and bleepy noise) Jack releases the confused Cam. He explains that he is an undercover government agent and gives Cam a note intended for Tony showing the location of the bombs. Jack tells Cam to hide under a vehicle until they're gone, then take the note to security. After Cam leaves the van, Jack cuts himself with his knife to convince Grant that the telephone engineer overpowered him. Eddie and the crew return to the van, and find Jack 'unconscious'. Eddie is angry that Cam managed to escape, and they drive off. As the van pulls away, Kimberly and Megan arrive at CTU. She tells the security guard that Tony is expecting her.

10:53 A.M. As Grant's crew speeds away from CTU, Jack asks how long they have. 'Four minutes,' replies Grant (see *Time Checks*, below). Lynne is angry that Palmer did not call her when the press conference broke up and she confronts Rayburn about why he kept Jenny's message from getting to the President. Rayburn tells Lynne that she does not want him as an enemy, but she immediately tells Palmer the situation when Rayburn explains that alerting CTU would expose Bauer's cover, and that as they now have CTU's intelligence, losses would be infrastructure and personnel. Palmer says those losses are unacceptable, and orders Lynne to notify CTU immediately. Michelle gives Tony the note from Cam about the bombs, and Tony orders an immediate evacuation of the building. This is why NSA wanted the data transferred. Tony receives a call from Lynne warning them about the bombs. Kimberly and Megan are escorted out of the building, along with other CTU workers. Tony sees that Paula is still working on the data transfer in Mason's office and runs up to drag her out. As they make their way down the stairs, the bombs detonate. From a distance, Jack and Grant's crew watches the building going up in smoke. Success! Rayburn informs Palmer that they were too late – CTU has just been hit. In Panorama City, a Hazmat doctor informs Mason that he has inhaled a lethal dose of enriched plutonium. He may have as little as a day to live. Tick, tick, tick…

CTU INCIDENT REPORT

Haven't I Seen You Somewhere Before?: Timothy Carhart (Eric Rayburn) is a well-known guest actor on American television. He is perhaps best known for his recurring role as 'Evil' Eddie Willows in season one of *CSI: Crime Scene Investigation*, playing Catherine Willows's seedy ex-husband. Sci-fi fans may recognise him as Lt Commander Hobson, a Starfleet officer who was horrible to Data in the *Star Trek: The Next Generation* episode 'Redemption Part 2'. He had even bigger hair when he played Sigourney Weaver's boyfriend in *Ghostbusters* (1984) – you know, the one who Venkman shouts at. Carhart's other film credits include *Witness* (1985), *Working Girl* (1988) and *The Hunt For Red October* (1990). Antonio David Lyons (Cam Strocker) appeared as Lawrence in *American History X* (1998) and can be seen in *The Sum Of All Fears* (2002). Sal Landi (Sgt Arroyo) was a regular in *C-16: FBI* with Eric Roberts and is occasionally credited as Frank Bronson, for reasons best known to himself. Scott Allan Campbell (Hazmat Doctor Porter) has played Sgt Martens in *NYPD Blue* since 1994.

Behind The Camera: Director James Whitmore Jr is the son of veteran actor James Whitmore, and it was an acting career that first occupied his time. Whitmore Jr began his career in the mid-1970s with gust roles in series such as *The Rockford Files*, *Police Story* and *Battlestar Galactica*. He would continue with regular work as a television actor until 1985, when he ducked behind the camera of popular detective show *Hunter* to direct several episodes while also appearing in the series as Sgt Bernie Terwilliger. Although keeping up with some acting work, Whitmore Jr has since devoted most of his time to directing, working on varied shows from *Beverley Hills 90210* and *The X-Files* to *Models Inc.* and *Buffy the Vampire Slayer*. He first worked with *24*'s creators on *The Commish* and his most recent work includes episodes of *Enterprise* and *Mister Sterling*, in which he directs his father.

Time Checks: At **10:16 A.M.**, Rayburn asks Tony to transfer the CTU database to the NSA server by **11 A.M**. Tony informs him that it will take until noon at the earliest. The bombs at CTU have a countdown of **12 minutes**. As they argue in the car park, Grant says they have **seven minutes** before the bombs go off, although a minute later the bombs are showing a countdown of **7:37**, so he was a bit out on that one. As they drive away from CTU, Jack asks how long they have before the bombs go off. Grant tells him they have **four minutes**. Now, a bit of anal logic discussion here on timings. When we go to the final ad break for this episode, the bomb shows a countdown of **7:33**. The ad break occurs at **10:49:26**. When we come back from the ad break, the clock reads **10:53:57**, a passage of **four minutes and 31 seconds**, meaning that the bomb countdown would have reached **3:02**, nearly a whole minute out from Grant's estimate to detonation. Are they inspiring confidence as crack terrorists? Suggestions as to where I can get out more will be gratefully received at the editorial address.

Fashion Police: Palmer changes out of the painful salmon-pink shirt and opts for a natty looking suit and tie ensemble. Much more fitting for a President in crisis. In fact, everyone in the O.C. is well decked out – Lynne Kresge looks good in a neat suit, and working for NSA must be lucrative as Rayburn has a nicely tailored suit too. If his bouffant got any bigger it would need a separate credit. Bob Warner is decked out like The Man From Del Monte, and has anybody noticed just how neatly trimmed his goatee beard is? Everybody knows only evil geniuses have goatee beards that neat, so we'll be watching The Man From Del Monte very closely.

The Perils Of Kim: Not a great week for Kim as she pretty much sits on a bus with an annoying brat for most of the episode. We do get the lovely moment, beautifully played by Elisha Cuthbert, as Kim talks about losing her mother. However, Kim displays a staggeringly selective memory when she tells Megan, 'We're safe here,' as they arrive at CTU. She's obviously forgetting that 18 months ago her mother was pumped full of lead there at the hands of Nina Myers. Rearrange the following into a popular phrase: last famous words.

It's Not Easy Being Jack: Do we think that Jack could have tried a little harder to put a spanner in Eddie Grant's works and stop the bombs at CTU? Perhaps he was secretly hoping that they'd succeed – after all, CTU was where Teri was murdered. He continues to show he's a seriously deranged man on the edge when he slices himself, quite convincingly, with a switchblade. Ouch!

Great Lines:
Hazmat Officer: 'I need all your clothes off!'
Mason: 'You're not even gonna buy me dinner?'

Death Count: The death count is bigging it up this week, with two dead terrorist bad guys at the bomb construction area, one cop going down in a hale of machine-gun bullets, and the shooter being dropped in turn by another cop. Add to that one telephone repairman with a permanently engaged line, and that brings the series total up to six after three episodes. Of course, there are unconfirmed deaths at CTU, but we'll have to wait until next week for that.

Trivia: Jack's sister lives in San Jose. Jack's priority code is 7117A.

DEBRIEF

Say it ain't so! CTU? Destroyed just three episodes in? As cliffhangers go, this is up there with *24*'s best, and brings back the series's Sword of Damocles – nobody is safe. Not only has CTU gone up in smoke, but the confirmation that Mason has less than 24 hours to live is quite sobering. This marks the first truly great episode of **Day Two** and one that really gets the pulse racing.

While we're here, just who are the NSA? With all these monogrammed security organisations knocking around – CTU, the FBI, the CIA, not to mention Joint Chiefs and other confusing chains of command, it gets difficult to keep tabs on who reports to whom.

Eric Rayburn is an employee of the National Security Agency, which was founded in 1952, replacing the Armed Forces Security Agency. The organisation's mission statement is: 'The ability to understand the secret communications of our foreign adversaries while protecting our own communications – a capability in which the United States leads the world – gives our nation a unique advantage.' In other words, operating out of headquarters at Fort Meade in Maryland, the NSA enciphers government communications going out of the US, and pulls apart any intercepted foreign communications. In light of recent world events and the current political landscape, the work of the NSA is more important than ever before.

The NSA uses a discipline called Signals Intelligence (SIGINT) to analyse data, a method that dates back to World War II when this method was used to break the Japanese military code, which revealed plans to invade Midway Island. The importance of SIGINT's contribution to the US involvement in World War II can not be underestimated.

Aside from the NSA's ongoing security work, the Agency also employs one of the largest Research and Development programmes in the US. Previous research projects led to the first solid state computers, and experiments with flexible storage media acted as a forerunner to the development of cassette tape.

Facts and figures fans may like to know that the NSA's annual electricity bill is $21 million. The Agency operates a blood donor programme and donates around 500 units of blood every month. The number of employees, both military and civilian, working for the NSA has never been revealed, and neither has the organisation's budget. However, in 1997, the operating budget for the entirety of the Intelligence Community, which also includes the CIA and FBI, was publicly revealed for the first time at $26.7 billion.

For more information on the work of the NSA, you can check out the Agency's official website at http://www.nsa.gov, where, if you're a U.S. citizen, you can apply for a job.

Pulse Rate: 110 bpm

Questions Arising:

- ? Why is Marie Barbie-Twin so suspicious of Kate Barbie-Twin's call from Ralph Burton?
- ? Did Jenny deliberately not pass on Lynne's message to the President?
- ? On whose instructions is Eric Rayburn acting?
- ? When will the *Sunset Beach* wedding have any relevance to the series that the rest of us are watching?

12:00 P.M.

Production Code: 2AFF04

Written by Remi Aubuchon
Directed by James Whitmore Jr

'The following takes place between 11:00A.M. and 12:00P.M.... Events occur in real time.'

Guest Starring: Reiko Aylesworth (Michelle Dessler), Skye McCole Bartusiak (Megan Matheson), Billy Burke (Gary Matheson), Timothy Carhart (Eric Rayburn), Michelle Forbes (Lynne Kresge), Sara Gilbert (Paula Schaeffer), Tracy Middendorf (Carla Matheson), Phillip Rhys (Reza Naiyeer), John Terry (Bob Warner), Sal Landi (Sgt Arroyo), Jon Gries (Joseph Wald), Scott Allan Campbell (Hazmat Doctor Porter), Scotch Ellis Loring (Paramedic), Douglas O'Keeffe (Eddie Grant), Jimmi Simpson (Chris), Freda Foh Shen (Doctor), John Sterling Carter (Field Reporter), Cliff Weissman (Rescue Worker), Michael Nagy (Secret Service Agent), Max Delgado (Hazmat Paramedic)

FIELD REPORT

11:00A.M. Tony takes charge amid the chaos of the CTU bombing, ordering Michelle to set up a triage. Paula is still alive, just, trapped in the wreckage of the stairs (although Tony escaped unscathed and he was right next to her – go figure…). They'll have to free her brick by brick, otherwise the whole structure will collapse on top of her. Kim and Megan survived the blast, and Megan has a seizure outside the building. She is rushed to hospital. Rayburn, in full cloak-swishing mode, assures the President that there was nothing they could have done. Lynne tells Rayburn that the personnel at CTU are dead because of him, and he warns her to keep quiet.

11:05A.M. George Mason is informed that he has around 12 hours before the symptoms of radiation poisoning start to affect him. Tony calls to inform him of the bomb hit, and that they are trying to save Paula – she is the only one who knows the encryption codes for the intelligence sent to the NSA server. Tony asks when he's coming back. Mason replies that he doesn't think he'll be coming back (and, frankly, who can blame him?). Joseph Wald calls Eddie Grant to tell him his location, which Eddie writes down. Jack reveals himself as a Federal Agent, and, after a shootout that puts the show's body-count up a few notches, heads off to find Wald, leaving the corpses of Eddie, Chris and, erm, the other one, behind.

11:16A.M. Jack calls in to CTU and speaks to Michelle. She tells him about the bomb, and he wonders why the building wasn't evacuated in time. He gives Michelle a progress report and tells her he's heading out to locate Wald. He also asks about Kim, who is currently at the hospital, awaiting news about Megan. A doctor speaks to Kim, telling her that Megan's X-rays have revealed a history of abuse. The doctor suspects Kim may be responsible, and says that the police can sort things out. Rayburn briefs Palmer on his recommended evacuation of LA. Lynne argues that until they know where the bomb is, an evacuation would be pointless. Rayburn argues that it would protect the President politically, but Palmer agrees with Lynne and refuses to sign the order as an evacuation would cause mass hysteria. Jack calls to speak to the President, but gets put through to Lynne. He accuses her of being responsible for the deaths of innocent people.

11:21A.M. Kate Barbie-Twin goes to talk to her father, The Man From Del Monte, to tell him what she's discovered about Reza being involved with Syed Ali. He refuses to believe her, as he hired his own investigator to check out his future son-in-law and that investigation turned up nothing. Reza offers to take Kate to pick up the lunch that Marie Barbie-Twin ordered. She hesitates, but The Man From Del Monte convinces her to go.

11:28A.M. Tony calls Mason, who is en route to hospital. He needs Mason's personal password. Mason asks how Paula is doing, but they're still digging her out. He asks the Hazmat officer if he's contagious – he isn't.

11:30A.M. Jack arrives at Wald's hideaway and begins to interrogate him at gunpoint. Wald was not aware of the nuclear device, and Jack asks him on whose instructions he was acting. A dog attacks Jack, distracting him long enough for Wald to lock himself in a secure room behind a steel door. With nothing better to do, Jack, after screaming for Wald to open the door, starts hacking at the walls with a pickaxe.

11:34A.M. Kim calls Carla to tell her where they are, and she accuses Kim of kidnapping Megan. Kim calms her down and tells her about the evidence of abuse. Carla agrees to meet her at the hospital and gets her car keys. She opens the door, only to be stopped by a waiting Gary.

11:40A.M. Jack gives up on his DIY when he comes up against a steel wall, and attempts to appeal to Wald's sense of patriotism by screaming through the door at him to try to get him to see sense. Somebody is out to destroy their country, and they're starting with Los Angeles. Wald sits looking at Jack on his monitor screen.

11:42 A.M. On their way to pick up lunch, Reza tells Kate that he knows she doesn't like him. She tells him not be ridiculous. Reza takes a wrong turn and explains that he wants to let Kate in on a secret. Showing how well balanced she is, Kate screams for him to stop the car, and he does, outside a house. Reza tells Kate that he only wanted to show her the house he's bought for Marie as a wedding present. Does somebody feel stupid now?

11:45 A.M. At CTU, Paula is finally freed from the wreckage, but starts to haemorrhage immediately and is rushed out to an ambulance just as Mason arrives back at work. He argues with Tony that they need Paula lucid for a few minutes so she can tell them the encryption codes. Tony thinks he's insane, but Mason orders the doctor to revive Paula there and then.

11:51 A.M. Palmer confronts Lynne for not telling him about the thirty minute lead she had on the CTU bombing, and he learns that Rayburn also knew. She offers to tender her resignation, but Palmer angrily tells her that he'll decide what's best.

11:54 A.M. Michelle demands to know what Paula is still doing there, and Tony tells her it was Mason's call as they need the codes. He has a crisis of conscience because he thinks Mason might be right, but is also racked with guilt as he was the one who brought Paula in at CTU and she never had a chance to do her job.

11:57 A.M. The President sacks Rayburn (about time really) and has him escorted from the premises. After much screaming and shooting from Jack, Wald finally opens the door. He only met the woman who told them to set the bombs at CTU twice – the second time, he had pictures taken of her. He throws a folder at Jack, tells him it's over and promptly blows out his own brains. Jack opens the folder and is horrified to find pictures of the woman who murdered his wife. Nina Myers. Tick tick tick...

CTU INCIDENT REPORT

Haven't I Seen You Somewhere Before?: While Paula lies under the rubble of CTU, it's perhaps time to look at the career of Sara Gilbert. Gilbert is, of course, best known for playing middle sibling Darlene in the high rating sit-com *Roseanne* for nine years. While playing Darlene, Gilbert played alongside Drew Barrymore in 1992's *Poison Ivy*. She would appear again with Drew Barrymore in *Riding In Cars With Boys* (2001). Amid many film and TV roles since *Roseanne*, watch out for a memorable appearance by the actress in *High Fidelity* (2000). Jon Gries (Joseph Wald) appeared in *Get Shorty* (1995) and *Men in Black* (1997), and was a regular in the TV series *The Pretender*.

Behind The Camera: Writer Remi Aubuchon is a well-respected theatre director who began his TV career in the late 1970s, working as a producer on the popular series, *The Paper Chase*. He begen writing for television with David E. Kelly's hospital drama, *Chicago Hope*, and contributed two episodes to the highly acclaimed mini-series, *From the Earth to the Moon*. He is a producer on *24*.

Time Checks: The Hazmat officer informs Mason he has around **12 hours** before he will start to show symptoms of radiation poisoning, meaning that Tony could be in for a pay rise come Episode 16. When Jack phones CTU at **11:16 A.M.**, Michelle tells him that the bomb went off about **20 minutes** ago. Rayburn's report on the evacuation of LA indicates it would take **one week** to evacuate the 9 million people inhabiting the city. Jack spoke to Lynne Kresge to warn them about the bomb at CTU **30 minutes** before it went off. Jack tells Wald that a tactical team will be with them in less than **two minutes**.

Fashion Police: Jack is starting to look a bit smelly and crinkled around the edges, so it's likely there'll be a change of

T-shirt on the horizon, while Mason gets out of his nice white zip-up jumpsuit thing and back into his regulation collar and tie. One thing that should be on everyone's mind is the answer to the question: just what the hell is Bob Warner wearing? All he needs is a Panama hat to complete his Man From Del Monte look, and that bad-guy beard looks like it's had a villainous trim between episodes. And while we're on the subject of fashion, why is everybody walking around the wreckage of CTU without hardhats on? It's good to see Tony looking a little rugged post bomb, but Michelle seems to have every little curl of her lovely hair in perfect place. Ooh, but that looks distinctly like a *very* bad wig that Nina's wearing in the photographs. Ouch!

The Perils Of Kim: Kim does well this week and is more a victim of circumstance than her own stupidity for a change. She should have bitch-slapped that uppity doctor for even suggesting she might be responsible for Megan's injuries though.

It's Not Easy Being Jack: Ah, poor naive Michelle. When she asks Jack what happened to Wald's crew and our boy replies that they're all dead, she sounds surprised. Anybody who knows Jack would have just shrugged. Later in the episode he sets animal rights back by about 200 years by shooting the dog (bringing Jack's personal body count for the series up to five – Goren plus Eddie Grant's crew). Do we think that Jack might be about to lose it big time when he sees the pictures of Nina? Let's hope so, eh?

Great Lines:

Hazmat Officer: 'How do you feel now?'
Mason: 'Like I wanna puke.'

Jack: (to Wald) 'You wanna blame the rest of the world for everything wrong with your life. Government's too big, they're too powerful. But here's a bit of irony for ya. You've got all the power now, Joe. Question is, what are you gonna do with it?'

Death Count: Oh baby, the death count ratchets up by the second this week. The initial death count at CTU started at 19, rising to 21 ten minutes later, before finally settling down at 27 by Palmer's count at the close of the episode. Add to this Eddie Grant, Dave and the one we couldn't care less about, an unfortunate dog and the suicide of Joseph Wald, the death count currently stands at 38, an average of 9.5 deaths per episode.

Trivia: Mason's password is Hendrix – he must have a fun side after all.

DEBRIEF

After the heart-stopping climax to last week's episode, this hour seems a little more restrained considering the enormity of what has happened to CTU. However, it's the constantly changing rhythms of *24* that make it such a pleasure to watch, so who knows where the heck we'll be in a few weeks' time. The wedding plot is starting to grate a little – it feels like a bucket of red herrings just for the sake of it, and it's time that somebody from CTU paid them a visit to justify the continued existence of The Man From Del Monte and his Barbie Twin daughters. The cliffhanger ending to last week's episode was always going to be hard to top, but they did it. Nina's back, and Jack's pissed.

Pulse Rate: 110 (plus another five for the cliffhanger)

Questions Arising:

- Is The Man From Del Monte trying to protect Reza?
- Was Eric Rayburn acting for a higher authority? Will we be seeing him again?
- What is Nina's involvement in the bomb threat, and were the pictures taken before or after the events of Season One?

12:00 P.M.

Production Code 2AFF05
Written by Gil Grant
Directed by John Cassar

> *'The following takes place between 12:00P.M. and 1:00P.M.... Events occur in real time.'*

Guest Starring: Reiko Aylesworth (Michelle Dessler), Billy Burke (Gary Matheson), Michelle Forbes (Lynne Kresge), Sara Gilbert (Paula Schaeffer), Laura Harris (Marie Warner), Phillip Rhys (Reza Naiyeer), John Terry (Bob Warner), Scotch Ellis Loring (Paramedic), Innis Casey (Miguel), Alexander Zale (Ambassador Shareef), Nicholas Guilak (Farhad Salim), Richard Gross (Fire Marshal), John Eddins (Agent Richards), David Ursin (Military Official), Tony Wayne (Agent Powers), Jacque Parson (Female CTU Worker), Ryan Moore (Kevin), Harris Yulin (Roger Stanton – uncredited) and Sarah Clarke as Nina Myers

FIELD REPORT

12:00P.M. As Michelle attempts to pull CTU back together, Mason checks on Paula's progress. They haven't been able to bring her round yet, and he urges them to work fast. Tony heads off to check up on a lead regarding Syed Ali having had dealings with a Middle Eastern businessman living in LA. Just after he leaves, Jack calls to inform Mason that Nina Myers was giving Wald his instructions. Jack has already informed Ryan Chappelle at Division and Nina is being transferred from prison to CTU for interrogation. Mason tells Jack to get somewhere safe and asks Michelle to set up a room for the interrogation.

12:04P.M. Palmer is still being briefed on possible bombing scenarios. Lynne informs him that the Ambassador of the country presumed to be responsible for Second Wave is about to land, and that Roger has arrived and is being briefed on Rayburn's dismissal. Gary finds Kim at the hospital, and tells her to leave before the police arrive. He'll let her walk away and not implicate her if she leaves his family alone. Seeing no choice, Kim leaves.

12:07P.M. A new NSA advisor, Roger Stanton, arrives to replace Rayburn, twirling his moustache as he walks through the door (figuratively, of course). Palmer is about to meet with the Ambassador, but Stanton advises against it – he is only there to discover what intelligence the US already has. Palmer acknowledges Stanton's concerns, but goes ahead with the meeting. Division calls CTU to let them know Nina is en route.

12:09P.M. Despite Mason's instructions, Jack arrives at the devastated CTU for debriefing. Mason naturally doesn't want him there with Nina on the way. Paula regains consciousness, and is able to give Mason the location of the decryption key for the data she sent to NSA. Mason tells her she's saved a lot of lives with that information just before she dies on the gurney.

12:17P.M. Reza and Kate return home after picking up lunch. Kate still isn't convinced that Reza is all he seems, and tries telling her father again, just as Tony drives up. He is accompanied by Agent Richards and has authorisation to interrogate Reza. Kate goes to fetch Reza. Marie is having her dress altered and Reza angrily tells Kate that Marie must not find out about the interrogation.

12:21P.M. Palmer, Lynne and Stanton meet with the Middle Eastern Ambassador, who informs them that his government has already arrested four Second Wave operatives and want to do all they can to prevent the bomb from being detonated. To that end, he requests all intelligence that the US has on Second Wave activities in his own country. Palmer is willing to play ball, but Lynne and Stanton are opposed to the idea.

12:25P.M. Kim calls Jack to let him know that she's OK. He tells her she must get out of LA , but she demands to know what's going on. Jack tells her about the bomb and that she has to go now. After his call, Jack continues working on his debrief report just as a shadowy figure in shackles is ushered into the building. It is Nina Myers. As she is escorted through the building, her eyes meet Jack's.

12:32P.M. Mason begins his interrogation with Nina, who puts a deal on the table. She'll reveal all her contacts in return for a full Presidential pardon. George tells her it won't fly, but Nina knows she has the upper hand. Mason leaves to phone Chappelle at Division and tells Jack, once again, to finish his report and leave. While Mason is on the phone to Chappelle, Jack notices him coughing.

12:35P.M. Tony begins to interrogate Reza, asking him about Syed Ali. Reza claims he doesn't know a Syed Ali, but Tony shows him the name appearing in Reza's personal computer files. How does he explain that?

12:36P.M. Ryan Chappelle calls Palmer to inform him that Nina Myers is asking for a Presidential pardon. After Jack completes his debrief, Palmer calls to let him know that he is preparing to offer Nina shadow asylum. Jack doesn't take the news particularly well.

12:44P.M. Kim calls her Vernon Kaye-lookalike music-biz boyfriend, Miguel. She tells him that she's in trouble and she needs him. He reluctantly agrees to leave his recording session. Jack confronts Mason about Nina's pardon, but Mason refuses to talk to him. Left in the bathroom, Jack discovers Mason's medication has been left behind. Even though he currently has no authority, Jack orders Michelle to reveal where Mason has been all day – he believes that his former superior may not be fit to run CTU. Michelle reluctantly agrees. Meanwhile, over in Soapland, Marie Barbie-Twin discovers the presence of CTU and has an almighty strop, which gets even worse when Kate Barbie-Twin tells her she hired the PI to look into Reza's background. The Man From Del Monte tries to intervene, but Marie says she doesn't want her sister at the wedding.

12:54 P.M. Miguel arrives at the hospital. He asks Kim what's going on, and she tells him about her problems with Megan and Gary and that her father has told her to get out of LA. Miguel pushes her on this point, and she tells him about the bomb. Miguel wants to leave immediately, but Kim won't leave without Megan. Jack tells Mason he knows about the radiation poisoning. He uses this information to blackmail Mason into letting him interrogate Nina, otherwise he'll report what he knows to Division.

12:58 P.M. Lynne consults with the President on the information exchange with the Ambassador, as Stanton barges in and tells them to look at an incoming news report. It shows the Ambassador's chopper, smoke blowing from its tail, crash-landing and exploding. It is expected there will be no survivors. Jack prepares to interrogate Nina. Tick, tick, tick...

CTU INCIDENT REPORT

Haven't I Seen You Somewhere Before?: Sarah Clarke returns as *24*'s arch-bitch, Nina Myers, having made a name for herself between seasons as an actress to watch out for. Prior to *24*, Clarke (sometimes credited as Sarah Lively) was an architectural photographer before beginning to work in the theatre.

She won an Outstanding Performance award at the Brooklyn Film Festival for her first short film, *Pas De Deux* (2001). She appeared in an award-winning advertisement for Volkswagen, and has also guest starred in *Sex and the City*. Clarke's film roles include *All About George* (2000), *Thirteen* (2003) and *The Third Date* (2003). Clarke is married to *24* co-star Xander Berkely. Innis Casey (Miguel) is very big in Mexico, where his single '*Dime Donde, Dime Cuando*' ('Tell Me Where, Tell Me How') topped the charts. He has recorded two albums, won awards and toured Central and South America, Hungary, Romania and Greece, despite knowing no Spanish when he moved to Mexico in 1999. *24* is his first major TV role. Alexander Zale (Ambassador Shareef) appeared in *Fire Fox* (1982) and *Showgirls* (1995).

Behind The Camera: Writer Gil Grant served as Executive Consultant for the Lara Croft-a-like series, *Relic Hunter*, contributing several episodes as a writer. As an executive producer he was responsible for the short-lived NASA-based drama series, *The Cape*, starring Corbin Bernsen.

Time Checks: Stanton provides satellite pictures that were taken over **one hour** ago. Kate Barbie-Twin tells her father that the wedding is in less than **six hours**. Lynne tells Palmer they can expect intelligence reports back **within the hour**, with updates **every 30 minutes** after that.

Fashion Police: Ooh! Give Tony Almeida a bit of natural light, and it does wonders for him. Look at that shot where he whips off his sunglasses outside the Warner residence. What a pity he spends the rest of the episode leaning over a laptop and looking mean across a table, much like he does in EVERY OTHER EPISODE of *24*, and, although looks may be deceiving, it also seems as if Tony and Agent Richards stopped off for some pies on the way. Either that, or the donut machine landed next to Tony's desk in the explosion. The less said about Kim's proto-Ricky Martin wannabe boyfriend Miguel is, frankly, the better, and Nina cuts a real dash in an outfit from the Cell Block H Spring collection.

The Perils Of Kim: A very bad week for Kim, although her dad isn't doing that well either. After Jack tells her about the bomb, she may as well have taken out a full-page ad in the LA Times with BOMB! in big red letters plastered all over it. Not a great move, Kimberley. This guide's advice would be to hook up with your cute boyfriend (even if he does look like Vernon Kaye), forget about the whiny kid and psycho dad and get the hell out of the city. It's not rocket science!

It's Not Easy Being Jack: This episode was always going to be a tough one for Jack, but when he isn't running around shooting bad guys, all he can do is flare those nostrils and stare (much like Tony) across the desks at CTU. Stupidity obviously runs in the family as he tells Kim about the bomb, breaking every rule in the book about being a secret agent. However, for pure TV electricity, the look that passes between Jack and Nina as she is brought into CTU is hard to beat.

Great Lines:

Warner: 'Ralph Burton is a PI. He could probably connect me to the Manson family if he looked hard enough.'

Mason (to Nina): 'You're not buying a used car here. You have to deal within the confines of reality.'

Death Count: If Palmer is to be believed, the death count at CTU is still rising (although everyone looked very happy munching down on complimentary sandwiches and not too flustered that half their buddies bought the big one), but with the unfortunate Paula being the only confirmed death this week, we're sticking at a total of 39 dead so far.

Trivia: Not precisely trivia, but Miguel has that really annoying Nokia ringtone on his phone. Kim should dump him immediately. Harris Yulin (Roger Stanton) is apparently uncredited for all his episodes.

DEBRIEF

A bit of step-down from last week's tense affair, but after five episodes it's perhaps time to take stock and regroup the troops. The wedding storyline is finally starting to pay off, and it's good to see Tony getting out of CTU. The niggling thing about the entire episode is that the destruction of CTU seemed such a clever idea, to remove that safe haven from our characters. Now it seems that nothing has actually changed and CTU is back up and running within minutes. What, in that case, was the point of blowing it up? The return of Nina is a definite shot in the arm for the episode, but please, can we have the interrogation now? It's time to take this season up to the next level.

Pulse Rate: 100 bpm

Questions Arising:

- Where is Carla Matheson?
- Is Lynne working for Roger Stanton?
- Is Stanton responsible for having the Ambassador's helicopter destroyed?

Production Code 2AFF06
Written by Elizabeth M. Cosin
Directed by Jon Cassar

> *'The following takes place between 1:00P.M. and 2:00P.M.... Events occur in real time.'*

Guest Starring: Reiko Aylesworth (Michelle Dessler), Skye McCole Bartusiak (Megan Matheson), Billy Burke (Gary Matheson), Michelle Forbes (Lynne Kresge), Laura Harris (Marie Warner), Phillip Rhys (Reza Naiyeer), John Terry (Bob Warner), Tamlyn Tomita (Jenny Dodge), Innis Casey (Miguel), Yareli Arizmendi (Mrs Naiyeer), Shaun Duke (Mr Naiyeer), Freda Foh Shen (Doctor), Bryan Rasmussen (Agent [Ed] Miller), John Eddins (Agent Richards), Michelle Anne Johnson (Nurse), Marty Ryan (Security Guard), Alicia Bien (Reporter #1), Pamela Stollings (Reporter #2), Harris Yulin (Roger Stanton – uncredited) and Sarah Clarke as Nina Myers.

FIELD REPORT

01:00P.M. Nina awaits her interrogation. Mason informs Jack that Palmer has signed the pardon, and they can begin the interrogation as soon as it arrives. Palmer arrives back at the bunker, and has to run the gauntlet of waiting press. He gives a brief statement before heading inside, to be surprised by the presence of his ex-wife. He isn't interested in anything Sherry has to say until she asks him if he ordered a military evacuation of LA. Palmer is taken aback by this, and Sherry asks him for five minutes alone. He says he'll call her, and consults with Lynne, who confirms that, to her knowledge, no evacuation of military personnel is taking place.

01:06P.M. Tony continues to grill Reza about his terrorist background. He asks him if he's heard of the Finsbury Park Mosque in his home city of London, allegedly a main centre for recruitment into Middle Eastern terrorist groups. Reza demands a lawyer. Tony refuses. In consultation with Lynne and Stanton, Palmer feels that the chopper crash was no accident and that it's possible somebody on their own side was responsible, considering the classified information on board. Palmer asks Lynne to set up an internal investigation.

01:08P.M. The pardon arrives, and Mason lets Jack begin the interrogation, hoping he's not making a big mistake. In silence, Jack enters the room, and shows Nina the pardon. She looks back at him, saying nothing. Eventually Nina tells Jack that the contact who knows the location of the bomb is in Visalia, but she won't give the name until they are there. Jack screams at her to give him a name, but she just smiles back. He grabs her by the throat and throws her against the wall. Mason has Jack removed from the room before he can do any damage, telling him, once again, to leave. Jack tells Mason that he needs Nina to believe he has the power to do anything he wants to her. He asks Mason to raise the thermostat by ten degrees and give him another five minutes. Mason agrees.

01:17P.M. Over in soapland, Marie Barbie-Twin is still refusing to talk to her sibling, but Kate attempts to make peace. She says they may have to postpone the wedding, but Marie screams at her sister to keep out of her life, like normal, rational human beings do.

01:19P.M. Kim and Vernon… sorry, Miguel, sneak into the hospital to find Megan, but Gary is standing outside her room. The doctor refuses to release Megan until her injuries are explained. Gary calls his secretary, and asks her to book two seats to Mexico City.

01:21P.M. Jack freaks out and Nina tells him the name of her contact, but she won't reveal his whereabouts until they are in Visalia.

01:23P.M. Lynne informs Palmer that Roger Stanton ordered a military evacuation of LA. Palmer has the order countermanded. Roger tells Palmer that he was only following Eric Rayburn's previous order. Palmer asks his secretary to call Sherry and let her know that he will speak with her soon. Gary finishes dressing Megan, and tells her they're leaving. Before they can go anywhere, Gary is called to the nurses' station to answer a phone call. It's Miguel, posing as an employee in hospital accounts. He distracts Gary long enough for Kimberly to get into Megan's room. When Gary returns, Megan is gone.

01:32P.M. Kim and Megan meet up with Miguel on the stairs. Megan begins to panic and doesn't want to leave. Gary is showing himself as the calm, doting father by screaming at nurses, and when Kim, Miguel and Megan get to the door, security has been alerted. They hide in a storeroom.

01:34P.M. Jack reluctantly agrees to Mason's wish for another agent to accompany himself and Nina to the airport. As they leave, Jack tells Mason to go and be with his family.

01:35P.M. Palmer confronts Sherry as to how she knew about the military evacuation. He tells her about the bomb, and she tells him that her information came from somebody in the loop within the defence department. There are people within Palmer's administration who want to control the Presidency. Reluctantly, Palmer agrees to provide his ex-wife with a secure line so she can find out more, and warns her that this had better not be one of her manipulations.

01:43 P.M. Reza's parents arrive for the wedding and find their son in CTU custody. Oops! Kate doesn't handle it particularly well (not at all well, in fact), and suffice to say, Mr and Mrs Naiyeer aren't overjoyed that their son is accused of being a terrorist. To distract the security guards at the hospital entrance, Miguel makes a run for it, stealing a monitor as he goes. The guards give chase, allowing Kim and Megan time to walk out of the front entrance. Unfortunately, Gary sees them from the window of Megan's room.
01:47 P.M. On the way to the airport, Nina attempts to play Jack and Agent Miller off against each other. She knows that once she's helped to stop the bomb, Jack will kill her. Will Miller be able to stop him? She also tries to goad Jack by saying that Kimberley has already lost one parent – how will she cope with losing a second? Jack takes this surprisingly calmly.
01:54 P.M. Reza's interrogation continues. When Reza won't tell Tony why he transferred the money to Syed Ali's account, Tony threatens to escort him from the house in handcuffs for his parents to see. Rather than put them through that shame, Reza reveals who really transferred the money. Bob Warner. In the hospital car park, Gary attempts to stop Kim and Megan, but didn't count on Miguel's skill as a kickboxer. Cool. With Gary out cold, Kim tells her boyfriend to get his car keys.
01:57 P.M. As Reza is reunited with his parents, Tony asks Bob Warner to accompany him to answer some questions. On board the van taking Nina to the airport, Agent Miller falls unconscious – Jack had drugged the water he was drinking. With a crazed smile on his face, Jack looks at Nina and cocks his gun. Tick, tick, tick...

CTU INCIDENT REPORT

Haven't I Seen You Somewhere Before?: Harris Yulin (Roger Stanton) is a very familiar face from both films and television. He previously played an NSA advisor in *Clear And*

Present Danger (1994) and has put in turns as countless doctors and army generals throughout his career. Fans of *Buffy the Vampire Slayer* will recognise Yulin as Quentin Travers, head of the Watchers Council, but *Star Trek* fans may not recognise him as the actor behind the make-up of Marritza in the highly regarded episode of *Deep Space Nine*, 'Duet'. Yareli Arizmendi (Mrs Naiyeer) has guest-starred in *Chicago Hope* and appeared in *Beverley Hills Cop III* (1994). Freda Foh Shen (Doctor) appeared in the U.S. version of *Cracker* and played Dr Norika Weinstein in *Silk Stalkings*. Her many film appearances include *Basic Instinct* (1992), the remake of *Planet of the Apes* (2001) and the voice of Fa Li in Disney's *Mulan* (1998). Michelle Anne Johnson (Nurse) played Hooker No. 1 in Kevin Smith's *Jay and Silent Bob Strike Back* (2001), just in case you were wondering.

Behind The Camera: Elizabeth M. Cosin has contributed episodes to *Snoops* and the 2003 revival of the classic cops and robbers series, *Dragnet*. She has also worked as a story editor on the woeful *Secret Agent Man*, and the not woeful *Law and Order: Criminal Intent*. Cosin also serves in this capacity on *24*.

Time Checks: Ooh, very bold. The episode opens with a shot of the clock on the wall in the interrogation room. It looks like it's showing the time as **1:01 P.M.** which is just about right. It takes around **eight minutes** for the pardon to arrive at CTU after Palmer signs it. Wow, that's some postal service. Another shot of the clock in the interrogation room shows the time to be **1:11:20 P.M.**, some three minutes after the pardon arrived, which seems a little quick, but let's not quibble. Jack asks Mason to give him another **five minutes** with Nina. At **1:21 P.M.** Lynne informs the president that the military evacuation began **an hour** ago. Palmer tells his secretary that he'll meet with Sherry in **20 minutes**.

Fashion Police: The *24* catwalk this week is a little bare, although the Naiyeers dress very snappily. They seem so nice, there's no way that little Reza could be a terrorist raised by parents like that. Could there?

The Perils Of Kim: Kim says, ' I don't know,' a lot during this episode. Why is she so dumb? We don't know. She tells Megan that they have to leave, but she can't tell her why. Well, she's been telling everybody and their dog about the bomb, so why not Megan? Oh, but full marks for finding a boyfriend who appears to be an Olympic gold medallist at kickboxing. Bravo!

It's Not Easy Being Jack: The fact that Nina isn't banging at the door begging to be let out of the interrogation shows she's probably just as mad as Jack. He strangles her, then practises his marksmanship on the wall behind her with a big gun. Do we think that our hero might need a hug? Jack proves himself to be the master of rhetorical questions by asking, 'Do you really think I'd sentence millions of people to death just for the satisfaction of killing [Nina]?' The fact that Mason doesn't reply 'Well, yeah,' just shows how polite he is. Jack's evil smile to Nina at the close of the episode shows he is one step away from a full-blown Dr Evil-style guffaw. You know, this new, mad-as-a-box-of-frogs Jack Bauer is becoming more likeable by the second.

Great Lines:

Mason: 'Jack, I don't have to remind you, the last time I let you interrogate somebody, you shot them through the heart.'

Death Count: Unless Jack has really lost it this week and put cyanide in Agent Miller's drink, our only casualties are the Ambassador, his mate, and a helicopter pilot, bringing up the score to a healthy 42.

Trivia: The Warners' doorbell plays the three-note NBC chime.

DEBRIEF

Much of this episode is mere window dressing to the main plot of Jack versus Nina. It's very annoying to keep cutting back to the wedding, Palmer, Kim and the kickboxing super-hunk recording technician. Couldn't everybody else involved just have had cups of coffee for an hour to give us a two-hander between Jack and Nina? It's good to see the return of Lady Macbeth herself, Sherry Palmer, who really does sit down and drink coffee for an hour. Her reappearance seems overshadowed by other plot moments, but we can expect a doozy of a catfight between the ex-Mrs P and Lynne in future episodes.

Pulse Rate: 110 (mainly for Jack's interrogation of Nina)

Questions Arising:

- Who is supplying Sherry Palmer with her information?
- Is Roger Stanton a lying weasel?
- Megan continues to ask the question on everyone's lips: 'Where's my mommy?'
- Are people within Palmer's administration involved with the plot to destroy Los Angeles?

2:00 P.M. – 3:00 P.M.

Production Code: 2AFF07
Written by Virgil Williams
Directed by James Whitmore Jr

> *'The following takes place between 2:00P.M. and 3:00P.M.... Events occur in real time.'*

Guest Starring: Reiko Aylesworth (Michelle Dessler), Skye McCole Bartusiak (Megan Matheson), Jude Ciccolella (Mike Novick), Michelle Forbes (Lynne Kresge), Laura Harris (Marie Warner), Phillip Rhys (Reza Naiyeer), John Terry (Bob Warner), Eric Christian Olsen (John Mason), Innis Casey (Miguel), Michael Cudlitz (Agent Rick Phillips), Michael McGrady (CHP Officer Brown), Christopher Murray (Dockerty), Anthony Azizi (Mamud Faheen), Shirin Sharif (Female Worker), John Eddins (CTU Agent Richards), Tony Wayne (Agent), Stan Rush (Agent Sloan), Demitri Fields (Officer Ken), Harris Yulin (Roger Stanton – uncredited) and Sarah Clarke as Nina Myers

FIELD REPORT

02:00P.M. Jack and Nina arrive at Warden Airbase. Nina tries to tell the agent who meets them that Jack drugged Agent Miller, but he is not on her side. Jack is given command authority and they board the plane. On board, they meet FBI agents Phillips and Harris. Phillips tells Jack he is there to ensure Nina's safety.

02:03P.M. At the Warner house, the kids (Kate, Marie and Reza) shout at each other over who told tales on whom. Kate is furious that Reza would put her father in the frame for this when he's obviously the terrorist, and Marie breaks up the fight. At the Palmer Compound, Chief of Staff Mike Novick is surprised to find Sherry there on his arrival, while Lynne fields calls about the disappearance of Ron Wieland. Questions are being asked, and Novick suggests leaking a story that Wieland left on personal business. Palmer agrees.

02:08P.M. Michelle informs Mason of Jack's drugging of Agent Miller. Mason is appalled, but there's nothing they can do about it now. The effects of the radiation poisoning are beginning to catch up with him. Novick is concerned about Sherry's presence at the OC – just because she believes there's a conspiracy against Palmer within his government doesn't automatically make it true. Palmer wants to use her to find the truth, and Novick offers to wade in too. Palmer directs him to start by looking at Roger Stanton – Eric Rayburn's boss. Jack finds himself up against the FBI agents as he continues to question Nina aboard the plane. They are ten minutes from Visalia, and Jack has her change into civilian clothing in the cabin.

02:17P.M. Mason calls his estranged son, John, and asks him to come to CTU as he needs to see him. John hangs up while his father is speaking.

02:19P.M. *Davenport Airport, Visalia, California.* Jack's team is greeted by a squad of FBI agents. Nina tells them Faheen's location and they prepare to move out. Jack is going to use Nina in the operation.

02:20 P.M. Novick begins to gauge Stanton's loyalty by informing him that the President has asked Novick to assist in the investigation. Stanton appears evasive, but agrees to let him have all the information on their best leads. Lynne briefs Palmer on where the best leads are coming from, he is aghast when she tells him that Jack Bauer is leading the team to Visalia and Nina is with him. In Visalia, Nina warns Jack that Faheen will commit suicide before he will let himself be taken. Jack tells her that she's going in first.

02:28 P.M. Tony calls Mason to brief him on the Warner situation. Reza has begun to talk and has put Bob Warner in the picture. Mason gives Tony authorisation to arrest them both and bring them in to CTU for questioning. Reza refuses to go, but Warner persuades him to co-operate. Marie insists on going with them. As they leave, Warner tells Kate to call their tax attorney and tell him where he's being taken, leaving his daughter very confused.

02:30 P.M. Palmer formally introduces Sherry to Lynne as they sit down for a private briefing to discuss the possibility of a conspiracy. Lynne and Sherry take an instant dislike to each other as they discuss certain meetings attended by Stanton and Eric Rayburn with the House Minority Leader. Lynne is aware of legitimate reasons for the meetings, but neverthless, they are going to keep an eye on Stanton.

02:38 P.M. Home alone, Kate logs on to the company's financial records and calls Ralph Burton, but gets through to Paul Koplin instead. She asks for his help. Sherry and Lynne have a nice girlie chat about their current situation. Sherry demands a little respect for being one of the people who put her ex-husband into office. Palmer overhears their conversation, and warns Sherry off. Jack's team arrives at Faheen's drugstore, and he orders Nina out of the car.

02:41 P.M. Nina enters the store and asks to speak to Faheen, as Jack and the team get into position. Nina is eventually shown in to see Faheen, just as Jack's monitor goes blank. Michelle relays information from a translator at CTU, but as Nina hugs Faheen, the audio goes dead. Jack orders everyone to move in, and after a shoot out, they find Faheen unconscious with Nina gone. Jack goes after her.

02:51P.M. Jack corners Nina as she attempts to escape through a padlocked gate. At gunpoint, Nina falls to her knees, her back to Jack. He places the gun to her head and tries to shoot her, but can't bring himself to do it. He handcuffs her instead.

02:53P.M. Just when we thought Kim had driven off into the sunset with Vernon Kaye and Megan, she returns to disappoint us as the trio are pulled over for speeding while attempting to escape the city. Mason has had his son arrested and brought to CTU so they can talk. In a rare emotional moment for Mason, he tells John that he is dying and gives him the number of a bank account where he has stockpiled a large sum of money. He then orders John to leave town. The police officer is about to let Kim and Miguel off with a warning, but as he walks back to his squad car he notices blood dripping from the boot. He orders Miguel to open the boot, which he does, revealing the bloody corpse of Carla Matheson. Oh, so *that's* what happened to her… Tick, tick, tick…

CTU INCIDENT REPORT

Haven't I Seen You Somewhere Before?: Jude Ciccolella (Mike Novick) recently appeared under alien make-up as Commander Suran in *Star Trek: Nemesis* (2002) and was involved in the super-heroic antics of *Daredevil* (2003) as McKensie. He is a familiar face from various guest roles on U.S. TV. John Terry (Bob Warner) has the dubious distinction of playing the dullest incarnation of James Bond's CIA liason, Felix Lieter, in *The Living Daylights* (1987). He also played Dr Div Cvetic in the first season of *ER*. Eric Christian Olsen (John Mason) will be seen in the forthcoming prequel *Dumb and Dumberer* (2003) when he will play a younger version of the character played by Jim Carrey in

Dumb and Dumber (1994). Michael Cudlitz (Agent Phillips) played Sergeant 'Bull' Randleman in the acclaimed mini-series *Band of Brothers* and also played Terry Phillips throughout the 1992/3 season of *Beverley Hills 90210.*

Behind The Camera: *24* would appear to be Virgil Williams first professional work as a television writer.

Time Checks: Phillips tells Jack they'll be landing in **ten minutes**. Jack says that as soon as they have a potivive ID of Faheen, they'll be inside within **30 seconds**. Kim tells her Aunt Carol that it will probably be another **four or five hours** before they arrive at her home.

Fashion Police: Nina changes into civilian clothing that has about as much style as the Teletubbies on a night out, but check out the nasty scars on her back. Did she get those in prison? And, come to think of it, when did Jack get the chance to change into that really natty leather jacket and purple shirt? He's looking good, and thank God he's lost that butch YMCA look.

The Perils Of Kim: Even with only about two seconds of screen time, Kim manages to wind up in the worst hot water yet, and this time, it's bloodstained. Not strictly her fault, it has to be said – if the kickboxing jock boyfriend hadn't been speeding, they'd have got away with it.

It's Not Easy Being Jack: Mason proves he's a master of understatement by calling Jack 'a little crazy'. A *little* crazy?! The man is a grade A whack job who would have Freud throwing away his pipe if he were ever on the couch. Jack's motives are also a little skewed on having Nina undress in front of him. It's very commendable, not wanting her out of his sight, but perhaps his former lover is giving him the hots in those prison fatigues. When it comes to the crunch, he shows he's still the tin man with a heart when he can't bring himself to splatter the brains of the woman he hates most of all in the world across the wall. Awww.

Great Lines:

Mason (referring to Jack): 'What can I say? The guy's a little crazy.'

Nina: 'He is going to put a bullet in my head before I can say hello, and then he's gonna turn the gun on himself.'
Jack: 'We'll make sure he doesn't turn the gun on himself.'

Death Count: With bodies going down rapidly during the assualt of Faheen's base, it's hard to keep count, but, including the poor girl who runs the shop, the FBI agent who smashes the door, plus three assorted varieties of cannon fodder going down from Faheen's group, that's another five gone in the space of less than ten seconds. Oh, and throw in one fricasséed Carla Matheson, and that brings the running total up to 47.

DEBRIEF

A crackingly good episode that brings the pace right back up to speed and chucks in a blinder of a cliffhanger for good measure. Having Kim absent for much of the action was a clever ruse to lull us into that false sense of security that *24* does so well, and then fire the bullet of Carla's death right between the eyes. The series as a whole is feeling much more rounded by now with the disparate storylines starting to compliment each other well – it was touch and go with the wedding subplot for a while. Finally, who's waiting for the cat-fight of a lifetime between Lynne and Sherry? Somebody get the popcorn!

Pulse Rate: 115 bpm

Questions Arising:

- Is Lynne being a little too quick to defend Roger Stanton?
- Why is Marie so keen to go to CTU?
- Why would Bob Warner call his tax attorney in this situation?
- Where did Mason get all that money?

4:00 P.M.

Production Code: **2AFF08**
Written by **Joel Surnow and Michael Loceff**
Directed by **James Whitmore Jr**

> ***'The following takes place between 3:00P.M. and 4:00P.M.... Events occur in real time.'***

Guest Starring: Reiko Aylesworth (Michelle Dessler), Skye McCole Bartusiak (Megan Matheson), Jude Ciccolella (Mike Novick), Michelle Forbes (Lynne Kresge), Laura Harris (Marie Warner), Phillip Rhys (Reza Naiyeer), John Terry (Bob Warner), Innis Casey (Miguel), Michael McGrady (CHP Officer Brown), Michael Cudlitz (Agent Rick Phillips), Anthony Azizi (Mamud Faheen), Al Sapienza (Paul Koplin), Fred Toma (Basheer), Maz Jobrani (Marko Khatami), Marc Casabani (Omar), Michael Holden (Ron Wieland), Brad Grunberg (Pool Guy), Terry Bozeman (Richard Armus), Harris Yulin (Roger Stanton – uncredited) and Sarah Clarke as Nina Myers

FIELD REPORT

03:00P.M. As Kim and Miguel are arrested, Tony arrives back at CTU with Warner, Reza and Marie. Tony is shocked to discover that Paula died. Bob Warner asks to speak to Tony alone, but is asked to wait in the interrogation room. Mason asks for an update, and Tony believes that Syed Ali is definitely tied in to the situation.

03:03P.M. Northwest Regional Operations Complex. Stanton questions Lynne about Sherry Palmer's security clearance and how happy Lynne is about Sherry being around. Lynne tells him if it becomes a problem, she'll say so. Sherry has received a call from a colleague of Ron Wieland – nobody has seen the reporter for hours. She asks Palmer about this, and he tells her the situation. She asks to speak to Wieland – she can make it worth his while to delay breaking the story. Kim, Miguel, and Megan are going to be brought back to LA. Miguel tries to convince Kim to tell the police why they can't go back. As they drive off, Kim asks the officer to call Jack Bauer at CTU, but he tells her she can have a phone call when they get to the station.

03:07P.M. Visalia, California. Nina interrogates Faheen in his native Arabic (Michelle translates for Jack from CTU through an audio link), but he is refusing to talk. Jack decides to take them back to LA, and as he tries to bundle Nina into a vehicle alone, he is told to back off at gunpoint by an FBI agent.

03:14P.M. Paul Koplin, Ralph Burton's superior, arrives at the Warner house to help Kate hack into her father's computer, to find out what dealings, if any, the company has had with Syed Ali.

03:15P.M. Stanton encounters Sherry being escorted through a corridor of the OC and asks Armus if she is cleared. Sherry doesn't take kindly to his tone and introduces herself. He asks what they are doing in that area, and Sherry tells him he'll have to ask the President. Armus shows her into the room where Ron Wieland is being held. Wieland is surprised to see her, even more so when she puts an offer on the table – make a statement to the public that he's fine, say nothing about the bomb, and he will be granted an exclusive to report from within the Operations Centre. She urges him to take the deal.

03:18 P.M. The delivery truck carrying the bomb has a blowout, and the three terrorists don't have the equipment to fix it. Fortunately a passing motorist offers to help. Aboard the plane en route to LA, Nina is still attempting to coerce Faheen into talking. He calls her a traitor and tells her he is not afraid to die. Before she is taken back to talk with Jack, Nina examines the edge of a plastic card she took from Faheen's store and slides it under her sleeve. She tells Jack that the plan to destroy LA was never revealed to her when she was approached, and that she feels Faheen really is prepared to die. Jack asks if there's any other way round him. Nina says there isn't and Jack sends her back to talk to Faheen again.

03:27 P.M. The tyre on the delivery truck is fixed and the helpful motorist goes on his way. Marko, the truck driver, watches a group of kids playing basketball – is he starting to have second thoughts? In the other squad car, Miguel has blabbed about the bomb. Neither officer believes him, but Kim tells the cop driving her to contact CTU and speak to her dad. The cop tries to get patched through to the FBI, but is unable to do so due to heavy communications traffic.

03:29 P.M. Sherry is forced to tell Palmer that Wieland refused the deal, and Palmer tells her that she can go. She tells David that he was right to remove her from his circle and divorce her after the election, but she now wants a second chance to prove she can be useful. Palmer agrees to let her stay, but can promise nothing in return for her help.

03:31 P.M. Driving the bomb truck, Marko finally cracks. He brings the truck to a stop, telling his colleagues he can't do this. He is shot by Basheer, who leaves the truck to remove the body. As he pulls the body from the seat, Marko turns out to be still alive, and shoots his former friend before he dies. Omar, in the back of the truck, is forced to leave the bodies of his comrades behind and drive to the rendezvous alone.

03:37P.M. Going through the financial records found in the computer, Kate and Paul find evidence of thousands of dollars being transferred to Syed Ali. As they search deeper, they discover a file in Bob Warner's personal directory that has a government tag on it. When they access the file, it has an auto delete program attached, but Paul manages to halt it. The file, it seems, is government encoded, but why?

03:40P.M. Tony begins to interrogate Bob Warner. Warner immediately tells him that he acts as a consultant for the CIA, and gives him a number to contact to verify what he says. Tony asks why he didn't reveal this earlier, and Warner is surprised at the CTU agent's naivety – he can't discuss what he does without clearance. His company acts as a conduit for information, to whom he doesn't know. Nevertheless, Tony stresses that the Warner company *does* have links to Syed Ali. As Michelle takes a call from the LAPD about Kim, Tony tells Mason what he has learnt from Warner. Mason says they're going to have to push a little harder than usual to find out what's going on. Michelle calls Mason over to inform him that the police are holding Kim, who has been charged with murder.

03:43P.M. Michelle calls Jack aboard the plane to tell him about Kim, and she patches his daughter through. Tearfully she tells him that she needs him there. In the background, Nina talks in whispers to Faheen, and Jack asks Michelle what they're saying. Nina has told Faheen that U.S. forces have stormed his village and arrested his family. Jack asks Nina what Faheen has told her. 'Everything,' she says and stands up, slitting Faheen's throat with the edge of the plastic card. As Faheen dies, Nina says she knows where the bomb is and demands to be taken to San Diego. Jack has no choice but to agree.

03:51P.M. Michelle reviews the transcripts of the conversation between Nina and Faheen, and has come up with a new name – Marko Hashami. She has the name cross-referenced and there is a connection to Ali. She tells Mason, who walks up to Reza and attacks him, demanding to know who Marko Hashami is. Tony pulls Mason off and drags him away. The cop who arrested Kim and Miguel demands to know what is going on. Worried that Megan may end up back in the city, Kim tells him the truth.

03:54P.M. Tony and Michelle share a doe-eyed moment. Tony tells her to go and get cleaned up and that they will survive the day. Palmer is discussing his ex-wife's presence at the OC with Lynne when Novick interrupts to alert them to a news report. Ron Wieland is broadcasting the story about the bomb on network television. They don't know how he got out, but Armus was responsible for security on the room.

03:56P.M. Kate walks Paul to his car as they discuss the possibility that her father may work for the government. As they talk, they are attacked by a group of men and bundled into the back of a van. Aboard the plane, Jack wistfully tells Nina about the last Sunday he ever spent with Teri and about what she took from him and Kim. Seconds later, there is an explosion and the plane begins to go down. Tick, tick, tick...

CTU INCIDENT REPORT

Haven't I Seen You Somewhere Before?: Al Sapienza (Paul Koplin) played Mickey Palmice in the first season of *The Sopranos*. Marc Casabani (Omar) played Omar in *Town and Country* (2001).

Time Checks: Mason tells Tony that **time is running out**. Oh, really, George, you don't say? Nina tells Jack that the bomb attack was planned **six months** before her arrest (presumably at the end of Season One). LA Dispatch has been unable to reach anybody at the FBI for **20 minutes**. Bob Warner has been working as a government consultant for **five years**.

Fashion Police: There's not a great deal to trouble the scorer this week, although it must be said that the three terrorists in the van look like they shop at Terrorists-R-Us. Maybe they could paint the side of the van with a colourful logo too? Tony looks much better now he's back at CTU, which is why he probably never goes out in the field: the subdued lighting gives him cheekbones.

The Perils Of Kim: Kim has a great start to the episode by being arrested for murder. Ever the mistress of self-delusion, Kim mumbles 'I can't believe he killed her…' after being arrested. Kim, Gary had 'I'm a psychotic knife-wielding maniac' written all over his face from **08:00 A.M.** Another nice move in telling the cop about the bomb, so the entire LAPD are going to know in five seconds, but it's hard not to feel sorry for her when she breaks down crying on the phone with Jack. She could have picked a better time to get picked up for murder though – 'Sorry honey, daddy's working.'

It's Not Easy Being Jack: After his brush with nearly killing Nina last hour, Jack seems a little more restrained this week; only one car gets the force of his temper with a smashed fist on the bonnet. You can just hear the combined mothering instinct of the female audience's hearts breaking when he tells Nina about his last weekend with Teri. Can somebody please give that poor guy a hug?

Great Lines:

Tony: 'Just tell me how hard I can push them.'

Mason: 'As hard as you have to. Stick bamboo shoots under their fingernails.'

Death Count: Three terrorists become one and Faheen ends up on the floor of the plane with a dodgy credit card sticking out of his throat. Michelle confirms to Tony that the final death count at CTU was 30, up three from the last count. With six dead this week, that makes 53 in total.

Trivia: Although Fred Toma, Maz Jobrani and Marc Casabani were all scheduled to first appear in **8:00 A.M. – 9:00 A.M.**, this episode actually marks their *24* debut. It's likely that they shot footage for the extended version of the first episode and this material was edited from the final cut.

DEBRIEF

Another case of treading water this week, with Jack cooped up on a plane for most of the time, and a cliffhanger that doesn't have that gob-smack element we've come to expect from this season. On a slight nit-pick point, if Michelle was supposed to be listening to the conversation between Nina and Faheen, why didn't they pick up the location of the bomb on the microphone when Faheen told Nina?

Pulse Rate: 105 bpm

Questions Arising:

? On whose instructions was Armus acting?

? Who are the men who attacked Kate and Paul?

5:00 P.M.

Production Code: 2AFF09
Written by Howard Gordon
Directed by Rodney Charters

> *'The following takes place between 4:00P.M. and 5:00P.M.... Events occur in real time.'*

Guest Starring: Aki Avni (Moshen), Reiko Aylesworth (Michelle Dessler), Skye McCole Bartusiak (Megan Matheson), Jude Ciccolella (Mike Novick), Michelle Forbes (Lynne Kresge), Laura Harris (Marie Warner), Phillip Rhys (Reza Naiyeer), John Terry (Bob Warner), Innis Casey (Miguel), Michael McGrady (CHP Officer Brown), Francesco Quinn (Syed Ali), Al Sapienza (Paul Koplin), Michael Cudlitz (Agent Rick Phillips), Michael Holden (Ron Wieland), Terry Bozeman (Richard Armus) and Sarah Clarke as Nina Myers

FIELD REPORT

04:02P.M. As Ron Wieland reveals to the media that he was held illegally inside the OC, Palmer confronts Sherry about the reporter's escape. She claims she had nothing to do with it. Mike Novick has had no luck in locating Armus, but shows Palmer security footage of the Secret Service Agent releasing Wieland from his holding room.

Jack's plane is going down rapidly, and amid the chaos on-board, Jack gives Mason co-ordinates of a crash site picked out by the pilot. Some kind of explosion has caused the malfunction. Jack appeals to Nina to give them the location of the bomb before they land, but Nina still believes Jack will kill her. Mason speaks to her, telling her the pardon from the President is still in place and Agent Phillips is there to protect her. Nina doesn't think that Phillips will be able to protect her from Jack, which obviously annoys the FBI agent, who pulls his gun on her and screams at her to tell him where the bomb is. Jack orders him to holster his weapon. The plane is not going to make it to the crash site, they're going down now. As Jack tries to tell Mason that the co-ordinates he gave are going to be incorrect, CTU loses radio contact with the plane.

04:06P.M. A statement of damage limitation in light of Wieland's revelations is being prepared by Palmer and the search for Armus continues. Palmer apologises to Sherry for jumping to conclusions about her involvement in Wieland's bid for freedom. She accepts his apology and urges him to tell the public the truth about the bomb. As Palmer wonders if his ex-wife has changed at all, Novick informs him that the plane carrying Jack Bauer has crash-landed.

04:08P.M. An injured Jack emerges from the wreckage of the plane and searches for other survivors. He finds a badly hurt Phillips, who tells him to find Nina. Stumbling around, Jack finds Nina, still in her seat. She isn't breathing, and Jack manages to revive her.

04:16P.M. Michelle shows Mason satellite photos taken prior to the plane going down – it appears a missile was responsible for the crash. As he looks at the images, Mason's nose begins to bleed, which arouses Michelle's suspicions. Tony badgers Mason about having moved Warner and Reza into a room together when they had agreed to keep them separate. Mason tells him to back off and Tony wants to know what the hell is going on. Mason finally admits to having radiation poisoning and that he will be dead by tomorrow. Tony is shocked, and they agree to keep this to themselves. Mason proceeds to interrogate Warner and Reza, taking no prisoners this time. He tells them about the discovery of the plutonium and the bomb, and the proof that a container was sent from Warner's company to Syed Ali. Mason offers immunity to whoever talks first.

04:19P.M. Kim and Miguel aren't happy to discover that they are being taken back to LA by the arresting officer – his captain has overruled CTU taking over the case as it's outside the agency's jurisdiction. Also, the officer doesn't believe them about the bomb as there have been no departmental alerts. Kim tries to explain, but it falls on deaf ears. Kim is convinced that her dad will sort things out, but Miguel suggests that maybe he's screwed up after all and they shouldn't rely on him.

04:21P.M. In the interrogation room, Reza starts to go a little crazy, asking Bob what is going on. Warner is evasive and tells him to sit down, as he's doing exactly what CTU want them to do. Mason and Tony monitor the pair's voiceprints – Reza's levels are steady, while Warner is spiking severely. Reza accuses Warner of having lied to him for years, and looks into the security camera, telling Mason and Tony that he can find out who authorised the container shipment to Ali. Warner attacks Reza, but is pulled off by security guards as Mason and Tony escort Reza from the room.

04:28P.M. As Jack and Nina await the arrival of Search and Rescue, Michelle advises Tony how far away the units are. She then asks him what's going on with Mason, outlining her suspicions that he has radiation poisoning. Tony confirms what she suspected, and

Michelle thinks he should step down from command. Tony disagrees, saying he will keep an eye on Mason. Michelle isn't happy, but backs down.

04:30P.M. Sherry and Lynne are one step away from a bitch-fight once again as the ex-Mrs Palmer gives Lynne notes on the President's forthcoming speech to the press. Lynne tells her to back off, and Sherry gives back as good as she gets. She tells Lynne she is there to help, and she's giving the notes to her as a courtesy instead of going direct to the President.

04:31P.M. Jack and Nina are leaving the crash site, just as a group of soldiers enters the area. As one puts a gun to Agent Phillips's head and fires, Jack assumes they aren't Search and Rescue. He asks Nina who they are, but she doesn't know. The pair flee into the undergrowth, pursued by the soldiers as a firefight begins in earnest.

04:33P.M. Kate comes to in a house, watched by her kidnapper. He reveals himself to be Syed Ali. He asks her what she knows about him, but she is unable to tell him anything. Ali takes Kate through to another room where Paul Koplin, tied up and naked, is being tortured. He screams that he doesn't know anything and they saw nothing in the Warner files. Ali's comrade switches on a nasty-looking sander and applies it to Paul, who screams.

04:40P.M. Jack fires from cover, Nina advising on the positions of the soldiers as they move in, feeding ammunition to Jack. With Jack occupied, she hides the final ammo clip. As Jack is now out of ammo, the soldiers move in, only to be picked off by a CTU chopper that flies overhead. As the chopper lands, Jack walks to greet the CTU force, but Nina picks up the discarded machine gun and loads it, holding Jack at gunpoint. She will kill Jack if the CTU agents don't stand down. Jack orders them to stand down and Nina demands to speak to the President.

04:43P.M. Megan's aunt arrives at the police station to pick up her niece and Kim shares a tearful farewell with her. The girl is going to Santa Barbara, about 100 miles outside LA and well outside the blast range of the bomb. Megan doesn't want to go, but Kim is just happy that she'll be safe, and says that she'll see her soon.

04:45P.M. Michelle informs Tony and Mason that Nina is holding Jack hostage at the crash site. Mason orders Agents Richards and Mackie to escort Reza to the Warner offices as he and Tony deal with the new situation. Reza is given a moment with Marie, telling her that her father may be involved with Syed Ali and that he's been used. Marie can't believe he would give up her father like that, and walks away from him. Reza is about to be taken to his office, but he asks to have a word with Marie first. Mason grants his wish. Marie tells Reza that a lawyer is on his way over. He tells her not to worry about anything, then informs her that Bob may be connected to Ali. An incredulous and disgusted Marie walks away from Reza.

04:52P.M. With Jack still at gunpoint, Mike Novick speaks to Nina, with Palmer present, and has CTU on another secure line. Nina informs them that she will reveal the location of the bomb in return for immunity for a crime she has yet to commit – the murder of Jack Bauer. Palmer consults with CTU, but Mason admits they have no weaknesses they can exploit now – Nina is their only chance of stopping the bomb. Jack tells the President they have no choice and should accede to her demands. All he asks is that Palmer ensures his daughter is safe and tells Kim that Jack loves her. The President agrees, but Nina will only gain her immunity when they have their hands on the bomb. Jack tells a visibly upset Palmer that he did the right thing, a sentiment echoed by Novick. Nina waits.

04:57P.M. As he is escorted to make his statement to the Press Corps, Palmer, within Sherry's hearing, acknowledges changes made to the speech by Lynne. The torture of Paul Koplin continues. Kate screams for them to stop. How can she tell them what she doesn't know? Ali believes her and immediately shoots the bloodied Koplin, ordering the torturer to kill Kate. With Jack still at gunpoint, Nina tells him it won't take long to find Ali. A calm Jack simply tells her that it isn't over yet. Tick, tick, tick…

CTU INCIDENT REPORT

Haven't I Seen You Somewhere Before?: Francesco Quinn (Syed Ali) followed in the footsteps of his world famous father, Anthony, and entered the acting profession. He is best known for his portrayal of drug baron Rhah in Oliver Stone's *Platoon* (1986) and has recently filmed a year on popular daytime soap *The Young and the Restless.*

Behind The Camera: New Zealand born Rodney Charters is best known as a cinematographer, a role he has performed since Season One of *24*. He has provided his services in this capacity for TV series such as *The Commish*, *Nash Bridges*, *The Pretender*, William Shatner's *Tek War*, and for the films *Car 54, Where Are You?* (1994) and *Kull the Conqueror (1997)* starring Kevin Sorbo. As a director, Charters has helmed episodes of *Hercules: The Legendary Journeys* (also starring Kevin Sorbo), *The Pretender*, *Roswell* and, of course, *24*.

Time Checks: Wieland tells reporters that he has been held inside the compound for **six hours**. Palmer puts it to Sherry that **ten minutes** after her meeting, Ron Wieland gained his freedom. At approximately **05:02 P.M.**, Novick shows the President security footage from **25 minutes** ago. The plutonium was found in the warehouse **six hours** ago. Mason's offer of immunity to Warner and Reza is on the table for **ten minutes.** At **04:28 P.M.**, Search and Rescue units are **12 minutes** away from the plane crash site.

Fashion Police: Between episodes, Michelle appears to have had a chance for a quick shower, change of clothes and moisturising session, and is looking all pink and scrubbed. She's changed her top from a purple blouse to a purple vest, so we're guessing she likes purple. Syed Ali strides evilly into the series looking like the Master from *Doctor Who*. He has a goatee that even puts Bob Warner's to shame, so he's obviously a bad guy. His weird-looking evil henchman has a nice line going in butchery accessories that Fred Elliott would be proud of.

The Perils Of Kim: There's not really a lot you can do to mess up things more than you already have by just sitting in a police station for an hour, and yes! Kim manages to get through an entire episode without having a single blonde moment. In fact, kudos to Elisha Cuthbert for her lovely farewell to Megan – it fair brings a tear to your eye.

It's Not Easy Being Jack: Ow ow ow ow ow ow! That *had* to hurt. Jack pulling a rather nasty-looking piece of wood out of his leg is one of the series most winceful moments (although just try telling that to the former private 'dick' Paul Koplin). Also, when you see the man grab a flare gun from the plane, you know that somebody is going to be flambéed very soon. Once again, Jack shows himself to be a patriot and puts the weight of the world further on his shoulders when he agrees to let Nina murder him.

Great Lines:
Jack (to Nina): 'This isn't over yet.'

Death Count: With bodies going down at a rate of knots this week, it's difficult to keep track of the death count. On screen, we see eight soldiers go down, with Jack dropping four, the remaining four being taken out by the CTU chopper. However, at CTU, Michelle informs Tony that seven hostiles were taken out in the operation, which doesn't tally. So, for the purposes of this category, we'll assume that Michelle's count does not include the four hostiles taken out by Jack, making the total deaths 11. Add to this the unfortunate Paul Koplin (ouch!), and our total series death count now rests at 65. Ralph Burton must be really glad he'd popped out for a doughnut when Kate called.

Trivia: In America, this episode was preceded by a viewer warning about violent content – um, no kidding.

DEBRIEF

The best episode of the season to date pushes the pulse-rate higher. This is classic *24* with just the right mix of action, twists, moustache twirling, suspicious glances and a great cliffhanger. Just how long they can keep Nina's involvement in this season going isn't clear, but there's at least one more episode of the magnificent Sarah Clarke to go. One thing that amuses amid this fantastic hour is that Jack and Nina look like they're running through the same woodland scrub in which Jack helped Teri and Kim escape last year. They could bump into themselves coming the other way!

Pulse-Rate: 120 bpm

Questions Arising:

- ? The question remains: who is Armus working for?
- ? Is Bob Warner really involved with Syed Ali?
- ? Who were the soldiers at the crash site?

6:00 P.M.

Production Code: **2AFF10**
Written by **David Ehrman**
Directed by **Rodney Charters**

> ***'The following takes place between 5:00P.M. and 6:00P.M.... Events occur in real time.'***

Guest Starring: Reiko Aylesworth (Michelle Dessler), Jude Ciccolella (Mike Novick), Laura Harris (Marie Warner), Phillip Rhys (Reza Naiyeer), Innis Casey (Miguel), Michael McGrady (CHP Officer Brown), Aki Avni (Moshen), Francesco Quinn (Syed Ali), Daniel Dae Kim (Agent Tom Baker), John Eddins (Agent Richards), Donzaleigh Abernathy (Assistant), Harris Yulin (Roger Stanton – uncredited) and Sarah Clarke as Nina Myers

FIELD REPORT

05:00P.M. Palmer delivers his statement regarding Ron Wieland's allegations. He admits that there is a current threat to the country, but then there are many threats made every day that are not always revealed to the public. He makes an assurance that there is no cause for alarm. Jack attempts to bait Nina about the things she has done, but she tells him they are done talking. Jack gets to his feet, telling her he doesn't want to wait around to be killed and walks forward. He pulls Nina out into the sights of a sniper who wounds her. CTU agents storm forward and secure Nina.

As Kim and Miguel are being transferred to a police SUV, Miguel creates a disturbance, causing his lighter to fall on the ground, and he secretly picks it up before being bundled into the back of the vehicle.

Novick gives Palmer word that Jack is unharmed, and the President orders that Nina be taken back to LA to share the fate of those she's endangered. As Nina awaits transport back to LA, Jack whispers something in her ear that either scares or surprises her. As Jack makes his way back to the CTU chopper, he examines a tattoo of a coiled snake on the arm of a fallen soldier.

05:06P.M. At Warner Enterprises, a handcuffed Reza is escorted to a computer terminal by CTU agents, and Agent Richards boots up the terminal. Ali's weird henchman, Moshen, is still trying to get information from Kate. Ali asks him why she isn't dead yet, and he tells his boss that he wants to be sure she knows nothing. Ali leaves the house to go and pray.

05:14P.M. Aboard the CTU chopper, Jack speaks to Palmer, informing him that he believes they were attacked by U.S. soldiers. Palmer is incredulous, but Jack goes on to say that the tattoo he spotted on one of the soldiers is the mark of a deep special operations unit, funded by the NSA, working out of Fort Benning under the command of a Colonel Samuels. He knows this as the unit tried to recruit him earlier in his career. Palmer is still dubious, and Jack goes on to say that the soldiers knew where they were and must have been given information from the inside.

05:15P.M. Michelle tells Mason she knows about his illness and gives her sympathies. Mason asks her what she's going to do tomorrow if the bomb doesn't go off. He tells her he once wanted to be a teacher, and he passed it over to work for the government for more money. In a rare moment of humanity, Mason tells Michelle to go and be happy in what she does.

Palmer questions Stanton about the existence of Coral Snake. He denies all knowledge of such a unit, but promises to look into it. Palmer proceeds to brief Novick and Sherry on Coral Snake and his intention to have Stanton arrested. Sherry believes this to be a bad idea, but Novick disagrees. Sherry urges them to find proof of Stanton's involvement, and Palmer gives his ex-wife leeway to find what they need.

05:21P.M. En route to LA, Miguel cooks up the stupidest plan in the history of stupid plans to try to get the officer to turn the SUV around. With the lighter he palmed earlier, he gets Kim to set light to his bandanna, which she shoves up front, causing the officer to lose control and drive the SUV off the road.

05:27P.M. Kim stumbles out of the wreckage of the SUV relatively unharmed – Miguel and the officer have not been so lucky. The officer is unconscious, Miguel is still with it but seriously hurt. Kim climbs into the front seat and releases her cuffs with the key before radioing for help. She then climbs in the back to be with Miguel.

05:29P.M. Moshen continues to torture Kate, cutting her ear with a scalpel when she doesn't respond. Jack and a team of CTU agents led by Agent Baker are outside and will be in place in 90 seconds. Reza and Richards are continuing to look through the financial records at the Warner building when Marie shows up. She insists on talking to Reza and Richards reluctantly agrees. She has had a complete change of heart and apologises for what she said earlier. That done, she leaves. Jack and his team prepare to enter the house as Moshen is about to blast Kate's brains out with an Uzi. Spotting an agent through the skylight, Moshen fires on Jack and his men, forcing them to pull back. Wasting no time, Jack has a shield brought in and they storm the room, Jack wounding Moshen. Kate is taken away, but they are unable to talk to Moshen, who has bitten down on a cyanide capsule.

05:38 P.M. Laying in the back of the SUV, Miguel urges Kim to leave him before the police arrive. With sirens sounding in the distance, Kim kisses her boyfriend goodbye and promises she'll find him when it's all over. She runs from the SUV, watching from a distance as medics arrive at the scene.

05:40 P.M. Jack talks to a traumatised Kate about what happened, and she tells him there was another man there, Syed Ali. Jack informs Baker that Ali is still at liberty. Sherry briefs Palmer and Novick on recent actions taken by Stanton. Orders came from him to have a 20-year-old communications network known as OPCOM reactivated. Sherry is checking to see whether Stanton contacted Colonel Samuels through this route, and Palmer has his Chief of Staff looking into the legal side of things so they can move against Stanton if need be.

05:43 P.M. Jack confers with Tony and asks him to run a background check on Kate Warner. He doesn't have to as he was with her a couple of hours ago and he still has her father in custody – her father is a freelancer for the CIA. Jack asks Tony to start going through everything from the beginning again so they can start to join the dots. He then asks Agent Baker to bring Kate back into the torture bathroom when she's ready.

05:45 P.M. Sherry provides Palmer and Novick with a still-active code for the OPCOM system, which Novick immediately goes to check out. Left alone, Palmer tells Sherry that she's doing an amazing job, which pleases his ex-wife.

05:51 P.M. Tony and Michelle go through the current information they have. In light of Mason's recent advice to her, Michelle suddenly tells Tony that she feels strongly about him and would like to go out some time. Tony admits to feeling the same way, but has been keeping his distance because of his experiences with Nina. They agree that if they get through the day they'd like to go on a date.

05:54P.M. Kate begins to tell Jack about everything that happened in the house. She says that the two men spoke to each other in Arabic, of which she understood a little as her family lived in Saudi Arabia when she was younger. Before he left, Ali talked about praying. Jack has CTU contacted for a list of mosques within a 15-mile radius. He apologises to Kate, but she'll have to go with them as nobody else knows what Ali looks like.

05:56P.M. Sherry calls Stanton, and warns him that Palmer knows about OPCOM and is having a warrant for his arrest drawn up. She tells him he doesn't have much time, and he mustn't reveal their connection – when all this is over, he'll have everything he wants. At the Warner building, Reza comes across the shipping order in the system, and realises that only one person could have had access to that file. Marie. As realisation begins to dawn, Agent Richards goes down with a bullet to the chest and Reza stands to find Marie holding a gun. He wants to know if the last two years have just been an act. She begins to cry and says, 'Reza, you really are very sweet.' Then shoots him. Tick, tick, tick...

CTU INCIDENT REPORT

Haven't I Seen You Somewhere Before?: Daniel Dae Kim (Agent Tom Baker) is a familiar face to fans of cult TV from his recurring roles in the *Babylon 5* spin-off, *Crusade*, and the *Buffy the Vampire Slayer* spin-off, *Angel.*

Behind The Camera: Writer David Ehrman was hired as a Programme Consultant for *La Femme Nikita*, bringing him into contact with *24*'s creators Robert Cochran and Joel Surnow. He was also a producer on the revival of *The Fugitive* in 2000.

Time Checks: At **05:15** P.M., Jack informs Palmer that their ETA for getting to the address provided by Nina is **15 minutes**. Baker's men will be in place in **90 seconds**.

Fashion Police: Kate's descriptions of Ali's ensemble are hysterical: black shirt with silver buttons and black pants. Yep, definitely the bad ass wardrobe of an international super villain. Where's the cloak?

The Perils Of Kim: Dear lord almighty! What kind of loser is Miguel to come up with a plan like that? Let's set fire to the car! What a great idea. It's about time Kim got round to dumping the jerk, even if he does do kickboxing. Kim continues to show us that she's her mother's daughter by running off into the trees to find out what other trouble she can get herself into.

It's Not Easy Being Jack: Jack is well in control this week – no mania, no intense stares at Nina. This is Jack the leader, Jack the soldier. We like it, but is it as much fun as Crazy Jack? Just to show he's still on the right side of nuts, he drags Kate back into the bathroom to answer questions standing next to the naked, castrated corpse of her private detective buddy. Was there any need? Finally, just what did Jack whisper in Nina's ear that scared her so much? Perhaps her fly has been undone since they left Visalia?

Great Lines:

Mason: 'Don't wait around for your life to happen to you. Find something that makes you happy, because everything else, it's all just background noise.'

Michelle: 'So you think I just want you for your information?'
Tony: 'What are we saying here? If we save LA from a nuclear bomb, you and I can get together for dinner and a movie?'

Death Count: Aside from cyanide junkie Moshen and Agent Richards (he had 'red shirt' written all over him from the moment he first appeared), we can assume that Agent Mackie was also taken out by Marie. The scores on death's door currently stand at 68.

DEBRIEF

Another great, action-packed episode that pulls the biggest twist so far out of the bag with Marie showing that she's not the dim Barbie Twin we thought she was. How so many people could be sucker-punched into believing she really was that stupid is one of *24*'s great strengths, and a reason that makes this such compelling TV. Bye bye Reza, we won't miss you! In other news, a big up for Tony and Michelle finally getting it on, and somebody should tell the production team that Tom Baker is not the best name to give a CTU agent. Where's the scarf and jelly babies?

With so much happening in the last couple of episodes, this is perhaps an opportune moment to round up the various knights and pawns who make up the *24* playing board, just so we can keep up with everyone.

Jack Bauer Since being recalled to CTU by David Palmer, he's shot a witness and sawn his head off, killed a dog and multiple terrorists, drugged a colleague, tried and failed to kill the woman who murdered his wife, seen off a squad of U.S. soldiers and been held hostage. He is currently attempting to locate Syed Ali. Jack is crazy, but definitely one of the good guys.

President David Palmer Palmer is attempting to uncover a conspiracy against himself within his government, allowing his ex-wife back into his life to help. A moral man who will be undone by those around him.

Kimberley Bauer She started running at the end of **8:00 A.M. – 9:00 A.M.** and hasn't stopped since. After avoiding death at the hands of her psychotic employer and death at the hands of her arsonist, kickboxing boyfriend, Kim is now running alone into the wilderness on the outskirts of LA. Certain danger awaits.

George Mason Dying from radiation poisoning. He has less than a day to live.

Tony Almeida Second in command of CTU and currently investigating the involvement of the Warner family in the Syed Ali affair. Has an attraction to his colleague Michelle Dessler.

Sherry Palmer 'Lady Macbeth' has just revealed her true colours, having insinuated herself back into her ex-husband's confidence. She now appears to be acting on behalf of somebody else, having connections to Roger Stanton, director of the NSA. An evil, manipulative woman who is not to be trusted.

Kate Warner An unwitting pawn caught between her family and Syed Ali. Jack Bauer needs her help as she is the only one who knows what Syed Ali looks like.

Michelle Dessler A highly capable CTU operative who appears to have no agenda beyond getting the job in hand done. Shares a mutual attraction with Tony Almeida.

Mike Novick President Palmer's Chief of Staff who saw him through his successful campaign for office. At this time, Novick appears to be acting in the best interests of his President.

Roger Stanton Director of the NSA who is acting for persons unknown, to help bring down Palmer's presidency.

Bob Warner Head of the Warner Corporation and father to Marie and Kate Warner. Previously suspected of links with Syed Ali, but in light of recent revelations now appears to be innocent. He also occasionally acts as a courier for the CIA.

Marie Warner Marie has successfully duped her family and friends into believing she is the sweet, innocent baby sister, when in fact she is the link between the Warner family and Syed Ali. It is likely she was recruited to Ali's cause at a young age during the Warner family's time in Saudi Arabia.

Syed Ali The terrorist activist who appears to be behind the plot to destroy LA. It is unclear whether he is acting for anyone else.

Miguel Injured. Last seen in the back of a wrecked police SUV.

Nina Myers Transferred back to Los Angeles. Who knows what the future holds for Nina Myers?

Pulse-Rate: 115 bpm (but up five beats at the cliffhanger)

Questions Arising:

- What did Jack whisper to Nina?
- Will Tony and Michelle make it to that dinner date?
- What are Sherry's motives and who is she acting for?

Production code: 2AFF11
Written by Gil Grant
Directed by Fred Keller

> *'The following takes place between 6:00P.M. and 7:00P.M.... Events occur in real time.'*

Guest Starring: Reiko Aylesworth (Michelle Dessler), Jude Ciccolella (Mike Novick), Michelle Forbes (Lynne Kresge), Laura Harris (Marie Warner), John Terry (Bob Warner), Francesco Quinn (Syed Ali), Bernard White (Imam Al Fulani), Steven Culp (Agent Ted Simmons), Faran Tahir (Mosque Guy #1), Daniel Dae Kim (Agent Tom Baker), Michael James Reed (Foreman), Edward Edwards (Colonel Lamb), John Eddins (Agent Richards), Carmen Mormino (Randall Sikes), Harris Yulin (Roger Stanton – uncredited)

FIELD REPORT

06:00P.M. Kim flees from the scene of the accident, hiding in the undergrowth from a searching chopper. At the Warner building, Marie prepares to leave, removing the hard drive from the incriminating computer terminal. Ali calls her, telling her to pick up the trigger for the bomb – it was left behind in a locker at Marko's workplace. He tells her to change her appearance. Ali terminates the call and enters the mosque to pray.

06:04P.M. En route to the mosque, Jack attempts to put Kate's mind at rest, but she insists on being told what's going on. Jack reluctantly tells her about the bomb and Syed Ali's involvement. They are interrupted by a call from Mason who advises Jack that teams are in place at the mosque. He also tells Jack about Kim's accident and that she's nowhere to be found. Jack angrily tells Mason to find her.

06:07P.M. Palmer has been unable to obtain a warrant for Stanton's arrest based on the evidence they have. Novick tells him that he may have to go further than he ever has in the past to be able to break the NSA director. Sherry speaks with Lynne, asking why she's being kept out of the loop on Stanton's arrest. Lynne says she has no idea, but if the President wants input from either of them, he'll ask for it.

Jack and his team have set up base across the street from the mosque. At this stage they have no idea if Ali is inside; he may have gone to another mosque to pray. Agent Baker thinks they're playing a weak hunch waiting for him to come out, and Kate offers to go in and look herself. She can cover her face so she won't be recognised. Jack is uncomfortable with this, but Kate insists.

06:15P.M. Stanton is locked out of the computer network and arrested for attempting to commit treason. Sherry contacts Palmer to enquire into his actions over the Stanton situation. He tells her that they are having him questioned, which she thinks is dangerous without evidence. Palmer, in no uncertain terms, tells her she is only there on his terms, and she should carry on doing what she's doing.

06:19P.M. Michelle apologises to Tony about putting him on the spot with her feelings, but he tells her that he's glad she did. Since Nina, Tony had made a decision to keep personal and professional separate, but now his hand has been forced. As they talk, Michelle gets a call – Bob Warner is turning violent. Tony enters the interrogation room and has Warner calmed down. Warner tells him that whatever Reza has told them is a lie. Tony tells Warner that his daughter, Kate, is with one of their agents, and she's safe. Jack briefs Kate on the location of the male prayer area within the mosque, and what to do if she spots Ali. They'll be waiting outside for her. Kate heads across the road to the mosque.
06:23P.M. Kate makes her way inside the mosque, bluffing her way past the doorman. She slowly walks through the mosque to the female prayer area, trying to get a good look at the men kneeling at prayer. Eventually she spots Ali, and escapes from the mosque through a rear fire exit, where Jack waits for her.
06:30P.M. Novick tells Palmer that Stanton's last phone call was made to a number in Langley, Virginia, where the CIA is based. Palmer interrogates Stanton, revealing all they know about his involvement in the affair and how he can be linked to Colonel Samuels. If the bomb goes off, Palmer assures Stanton he will be executed, but if he talks now, he is prepared to offer full immunity. Stanton claims he knows nothing.
06:32P.M. Jack briefs the team outside the mosque, who take their positions around the building. Kate and Jack take up a vantage point across the street, waiting for the service to end. Jack tells Kate that what she did was very brave.
06:35P.M. Kim makes her way through the bush, alone. She thinks she is being followed, and notices a cougar stalking her. Running away from the cat, Kim is caught in a hunter's trap. As she attempts to free herself, the cougar emerges from the trees and looks down at her from an outcrop.
06:41P.M. Palmer leaves the OC compound to attend a covert

meeting with a Secret Service Agent, Ted Simmons. The President enquires as to his special ops background, and asks if he knew of Roger Stanton's arrest. Simmons says that he did. Palmer asks Ted to interrogate and extract information from Stanton. He has the authorisation to go as far as he needs to.

At CTU, Michelle breaks the news that Reza Nyer and their agents have been killed at the Warner building. Tony is aghast when Marie Warner appears to be the only suspect. He immediately calls Jack to inform him of the news and that he should treat Kate as an unknown – she may be involved. Jack doesn't think so.

A disguised Marie arrives at Marko's workplace. She tells the foreman that she's Marko's girlfriend, and needs something from his locker. The foreman isn't going to help, until Marie offers to make it worth his while and leads him seductively into his office.

06:52P.M. Simmons begins to interrogate Stanton using a defibrillator to shock him. Stanton says he knows nothing, and the interrogation continues. Palmer watches on a security monitor.

06:53P.M. Tony gives Warner the news that Reza has been killed and they believe Marie is responsible. Warner thinks they are attempting to trick him, and Tony slides a folder of evidence across the table for him to look through.

06:55P.M. As darkness falls, people begin to file from the mosque. Kate fails to spot Ali in the crowd. Jack asks if she's telling the truth, which upsets her. He orders the team to storm the building. As they search through the mosque, Jack and Baker find a burning corpse – the clothes match those of Ali. Jack has the team stand down as they have their man, who Baker confirms is dead. Speaking on the phone, Jack suddenly notices that the clothes on the charred corpse are too small. Ali is still in the building. Tick tick tick...

CTU INCIDENT REPORT

Haven't I Seen You Somewhere Before?: Bernard White (Imam Al Fulani) is a veteran of U.S. soaps, having done stints on *Days of Our Lives*, *Santa Barbara* and *General Hospital*. His film work includes *The Scorpion King* (2002), *Pay It Forward* (2000) and *City Of Angels* (1998). Steven Culp (Agent Ted Simmons) had a brush with presidential affairs previously, taking on the role of Robert Kennedy in *Thirteen Days* (2000). For sci-fi fans, his greatest claim to fame is playing Commander Martin Madden, the new First Officer of the USS *Enterprise* in *Star Trek: Nemesis* (2002). Unfortunately, his scenes were beamed on to the cutting room floor.

Behind The Camera: Director Fred Keller (also known as Frederick King Keller) has had a varied career in television. As a director he has worked on *Seaquest DSV*, *Nash Bridges*, *The Pretender*, *Roswell* and *Angel*, and also provided the storyline for the TV movie *Columbo: Columbo Goes to College* in 1991. He is currently a producer on the well-received cop show *Boomtown*, starring Donnie Wahlberg.

Time Checks: At **06:32 P.M.**, Jack states it is **19 minutes** to the end of the prayer service. At **06:35 P.M.**, Jack tells Kate the service will be over in **17 minutes**. At around **06:57 P.M.**, Jack tells the leader of the mosque that **15 minutes** ago they'd had a positive sighting of Syed Ali.

Fashion Police: Lots of testosterone on show this week from the assembled CTU forces around the mosque. Look at Agent Doctor Who… sorry, Tom Baker, hardly breaking a sweat as he runs around in his swish combat fatigues. Wonder where he gets the hair gel? Kate is forced to go *sans* shoes for her trip inside the mosque, and it's probably best not to ask where they got the yashmak. Jack's eye for sartorial matters is good, spotting the clothing size on 'Ali's' body. Perhaps being an international super terrorist doesn't give you time to shop for threads that fit. Marie decides to go from 'cute little Barbie doll' to 'Hi, I'm an enormous slut' in the space of five minutes. Nice wig too.

The Perils Of Kim: Kim brings a new meaning to the expression 'hot pussy' as she gets chased through the woods by a very big, scary cat. We should also pity poor Elisha Cuthbert who, without the boyfriend in tow, is reduced to running. And running. And running. And falling over.

It's Not Easy Being Jack: Now that Jack's got a hot blonde babe to look after, he's turned all caring and sharing. Fox executives did hint of a possible tryst for Jack and Kate, and with 12 hours to go, the clock is ticking. One word of warning to Kate – if you find yourself in a dark back room at CTU, say around **07:45 A.M.** tomorrow morning, run away.

Great Lines:

Palmer (to Sherry): 'You're not a member of my staff. You're not a government employee and you're not my wife.'

Death Count: With only one char-grilled corpse on the menu this hour, that clicks the counter up to 69.

Trivia: Elisha Cuthbert received an injury to her hand from the cougar used while filming this episode. Showing her wound on the U.S. talk show *Regis and Kelly*, Elisha was unable to say how she'd received the injury as it would spoil the upcoming storyline.

DEBRIEF

Another back-burner episode that has everybody off doing their own thing – in Marie's case, quite literally. The most intrigue comes from the situation instigated by Palmer in having Roger Stanton tortured for information. This raises the question of just how far people should go to protect their country, and if their actions put them on the level of those they seek to bring to justice. Finally, would it be possible for Tony and Michelle to nip off to the broom cupboard for ten minutes and then just get on with their lives? We know you're going to grab a movie, but please, there's a bomb to find.

Pulse-Rate: 105 bpm

QUESTIONS ARISING

- Is Stanton telling the truth?
- Where is Syed Ali?

8:00 P.M.

Production Code: 2AFF12
Written by Evan Katz
Directed by Fred Keller

> *'The following takes place between 7:00P.M. and 8:00P.M.... Events occur in real time.'*

Guest Starring: Reiko Aylesworth (Michelle Dessler), Jude Ciccolella (Mike Novick), Michelle Forbes (Lynne Kresge), Laura Harris (Marie Warner), John Terry (Bob Warner), Francesco Quinn (Syed Ali), Kevin Dillon (Lonnie McRae), Daniel Dae Kim (Agent Tom Baker), Bernard White (Imam Al Fulani), Steven Culp (Agent Ted Simmons), Val Lauren (Agent Randy Murdoch), Dane Northcutt (Trap Door Agent), Ike Bram (Fareed), Marc Casabani (Omar), R.J. Fenske (Asad), Shaheen Vaaz (Ali's Wife), Harris Yulin (Roger Stanton – uncredited)

FIELD REPORT

07:00P.M. Jack and the CTU continue to search for Ali throughout the mosque. Jack has a fragment of burned paper retrieved from Ali's clothing sent to CTU for analysis. He then talks to the leader of the mosque, who tells Jack that if Ali is guilty of the crimes they claim he is, he is guilty in the eyes of Allah as well. As Kate waits around to make the final identification of Ali, an agent informs Jack they've found a trapdoor that isn't on the plans of the building. Jack examines the door – it leads down into a dark passageway. He tells the agent he is heading into the corridor alone – if more go, it could scare Ali into taking his life with a cyanide pill – but they should have a team standing by at the base of the ladder. He takes the agent's baton and climbs down.

07:04P.M. Driving through Los Angeles, Marie receives a call from Ali. He tells her that the plan has changed. She is to proceed to the rendezvous point. If he is not there in half an hour, she knows what to do. As he finishes the call, he hears a noise and goes to investigate. Jack is waiting for him, and wrestles him to the ground, forcing the baton into Ali's mouth to prevent him from biting down on the cyanide. The CTU team arrives to assist and after a struggle, Jack manages to remove the cyanide pill intact. Jack throws the mobile phone at Baker and asks him to find out who Ali was speaking to.

07:05P.M. Mason talks to Bob Warner about Marie. Warner feels there must be some mistake in their evidence incriminating his daughter. Mason tells him it's black and white, and wonders if this might help to explain any odd behaviour in Marie from recent years. Warner recalls that shortly after his wife died, Marie disappeared travelling for about four weeks to get some space. They received a letter saying she was OK, and when she finally returned, she had suddenly become very apolitical. Mason believes this is a sure sign that she was compromised. Michelle interrupts the interview to show Mason a scan of the paper sent over by Jack. It has some numbers on it, which they can't yet read, but they've called in a computer expert, Randy Murdoch, to assist.

07:09P.M. Simmons continues with his interrogation of Stanton, viewed on the monitor by President Palmer. Novick informs Palmer that Jack Bauer is now interrogating Syed Ali. Palmer muses on something that Agent Simmons told him – that Stanton received the same training as the agent himself in resisting torture. But, as Palmer concludes, everybody breaks.

07:14P.M. Mason berates Tony for devoting time to searching for Kim. He is a CTU resource, Kim is now outside the blast radius, the rest of Los Angeles isn't, and that's where his priorities should lie.

07:15P.M. Kim is still trapped in the hunter's snare, and it is now dark and cold. She hears somebody approaching through the trees and moves to hide behind a rock. A young man carrying a rifle emerges from the undergrowth and spots her. He asks her what she's doing all the way out there, but she's evasive. The hunter releases her from the snare.

07:17P.M. As Kate watches CTU agents rushing back and forth, Jack violently interrogates Ali. Ali is safe in the knowledge that he was going to die today anyway, and refuses to talk.

The hunter bandages Kim's foot and wonders how they're going to get her to the nearest ranger station. Kim doesn't want to go there, so he offers to put a roof over her head for the night.

The leader of the mosque enters the room to appeal to Ali. He says the Koran forbids the murder of innocents, but Ali says he has a different interpretation of the holy text. The leader leaves the room, but tells Jack, who is supervising the setting up of monitors, that he wants to try again. Jack tells him he can't be involved in what will happen next, and has the man taken upstairs. Baker gives Jack the last number called by Ali, and Kate overhears. She thinks it's impossible, as it's her sister's mobile, and demands to know what's going on. Jack tells her about Reza's murder, and that they believe Marie is the prime suspect. Kate refuses to believe him, and Jack tells her the only way to find out is if she calls Marie's phone. If Marie answers, she must keep her on the phone long enough for them to trace her. Jack asks Baker to make it look like Kate is calling from her own mobile.

07:28 P.M. Kate calls Marie from the mosque and attempts to keep her on the phone. A very calm Marie tells her that they know about Reza, and terminates the call, throwing her phone out of the car window. They managed to get a fix on her location, and Jack orders the area to be closed down. Kate breaks down in tears. All Jack can do is tell her he's sorry.

07:31 P.M. At CTU, Michelle informs Tony that they are still waiting to hear from the ranger station about Kim. Meanwhile, Murdoch has made progress with the burnt paper, uncovering 'N34'. He still has some more markings to uncover, and Tony sets Michelle to finding some kind of context for the writing on the paper.

07:32 P.M. A copy of the burnt paper is sent back to Jack, who demands to know from Ali what 'N34' means. Ali, once again, refuses to talk. Baker informs Jack that the live link is up, and Jack switches on monitors that have been set up in the room. They show Ali's wife and two children being tied to chairs by masked men. Ali is shocked and Jack tells him that the men will kill his family if he doesn't reveal the location of the bomb.

07:38 P.M. Novick informs Palmer that Jack Bauer is currently threatening to have Syed Ali's family executed. Palmer is shocked – have civilians ever been threatened in this way in the past? Novick believes that the end justifies the means, but Palmer cannot understand how things have come to this. Ali watches in horror as his family is tied up. Jack tells the terrorist that he knows what it's like to have a loved one killed in front of you, but he will give the order. Ali claims he is doing Allah's work. An agent enters the room – Palmer wishes to speak to Jack. The President cannot allow Jack to proceed with this action, but Jack protests it is the only way.

Palmer forbids him to murder Ali's family, and his decision is final. Jack carries on speaking into the phone after the call has finished, duping Ali into thinking that the President has just given authorisation to proceed. Ali looks, horrified, at a close up of his son's face.

07:43 P.M. Novick is fielding calls on the whereabouts of Roger Stanton. Lynne comes to him with information. Although Sherry Palmer claimed that she had never met Roger Stanton until today, Lynne has evidence that they have had regular meetings over the last six months. Novick is not entirely shocked, and Lynne tells him that she is about to have a meeting off-site with her source. Novick advises her to go ahead, but to be careful.

07:45 P.M. Jack gives Ali one last chance to reveal the location of the bomb. Ali again refuses, and Jack gives the order for the soldiers to kill his eldest son, Asad. The soldier fires and Ali screams in rage. Jack will spare the rest of his family if he tells them where the bomb is. Ali he still refuses.

07:51 P.M. Lynne arrives for her meeting off-site (in a scary Scooby Doo neighbourhood it seems). Instead of the person she was supposed to meet, Lynne is surprised to find Sherry Palmer waiting for her. Sherry tells her to back off and that the people who are acting against the President are trying to set her up. Lynne believes that Sherry has set up the whole thing just to demonstrate how powerful she is.

Jack pushes Ali further. He can't bring Asad back from the dead, but he can save his youngest son if he simply tells them where the bomb is. Ali refuses, and Jack gives the order, but at the last second Ali screams that he will tell them. The bomb is at Norton airfield, and they are going to fly the bomb over downtown LA and then detonate. Jack immediately calls Mason and gives him the information. Mason has CTU units mobilised to the airfield. Ali is led screaming from the mosque, vowing to revenge himself on Jack. Kate accuses Jack of being worse than the terrorists, but then she sees Ali's son being helped up on the monitor, unharmed. It was all faked. Jack asks Kate to accompany them to the airfield in case she has to talk to her sister. Marie arrives at the airfield and delivers the bomb trigger. It is placed in the bomb, which activates. Omar looks at Marie and says: 'Now we pray.' Tick tick tick…

CTU INCIDENT REPORT

Haven't I Seen You Somewhere Before?: Kevin Dillon (Lonnie McRae) is the brother of actor Matt Dillon and a reasonably well-known face from his many film roles. He is perhaps best known as John Densmore in Oliver Stone's *The Doors* (1991). He also played Officer Neil Baker on a semi-regular basis in *NYPD Blue*. Dane Northcutt (Trap Door Agent) played Hicks in *Tigerland* (2000).

Behind The Camera: Writer Evan Katz has also contributed episodes to the military legal drama *JAG*, and was the creator of the short-lived series *Special Unit 2*. He also serves as a producer for *24*.

Time Checks: Ali tells Marie to wait at the rendezvous point for **half an hour**. Jack tells Kate that Reza was murdered **an hour and a half** ago.

Fashion Police: Sherry Palmer attends her secret meeting with Lynne looking like she's stepped out of a Yardley commercial, circa 1970, and, if we didn't know better, we'd think Bob Warner's beard had transformed into a big false one.

The Perils Of Kim: Do we trust the strange hermit hunter with whom Kim has just agreed to go and spend the night in his unique fixer-upper shack in the middle of nowhere? We're sort of coming down on the side of no, but then, we're tucked up reading this in bed with a mug of cocoa. In Kim's situation, with the cops out looking for her on one side, and a forest full of cougars on the other, she's probably made the right decision for once.

It's Not Easy Being Jack: Blimey! Ol' Jack really pushes things hard this week. The baton-down-the-gob-trick is only the beginning of what turns out to be Jack's most consistently violent hour to date – even the poor little doggy and the head-sawing incident aren't quite on a par with the sadistic tendencies displayed here. It's a necessary deception to show he's prepared to go all the way to get the job done and convince Ali (and the audience) that he will kill the children. He's still softening when Kate's around, and just look at her face when she realises it was all some hilarious candid camera stunt. Is it possible she's lining herself up to become Kim's new stepmom? Could the Bauer household take that much blonde?

Great Lines:

Palmer: 'Everyone breaks eventually.'

Ali: 'I woke up today knowing I would die.'
Jack: 'I can make you die with more pain than you ever imagined.'
Ali: 'Then I will have that much more pleasure in Paradise.'

Jack (to Ali): 'The only way you're gonna die today is if I kill ya.'

Death Count: Ooh Jack, you're a wily little trickster. Obviously this is a good thing, but just when we thought we had another addition to death row, it turns out it was all a ruse. Yay! for Jack though.

Trivia: Marie Warner's cell phone number is 555 2130.

DEBRIEF

In the U.S., this episode was preceded by a viewer discretion warning for violent content. And they weren't kidding, were they? Between Stanton being electrocuted to within an inch of his life and Ali having the crap kicked out of him, this pushes *24* into a whole different ball game. Kiefer Sutherland is pumping out the energy like there's no tomorrow, and somebody had better tell the guy that there's another 12 hours to get through.

Palmer's moral outrage at what Jack is about to do to Ali's family is a bit hard to swallow. He's quite happy kidnapping reporters and frying his NSA director seemingly in order to protect his office, but when it comes to protecting the millions of innocents in LA for real, he's a pussy. Tough times are ahead for that man – but this is *24*, so what else is new?

Pulse-Rate: 120 bpm

Questions Arising:

- Will Roger Stanton break?
- What fate awaits Syed Ali?
- Is Sherry Palmer telling the truth?
- How long can Mason stay in command at CTU?

9:00 P.M.

Production Code: 2AFF13
Written by Maurice Hurley
Directed by Jon Cassar

> *'The following takes place between 8:00P.M. and 9:00P.M.... Events occur in real time.'*

Guest Starring: Reiko Aylesworth (Michelle Dessler), Jude Ciccolella (Mike Novick), Michelle Forbes (Lynne Kresge), Laura Harris (Marie Warner), Kevin Dillon (Lonnie McRae), Daniel Dae Kim (Agent Tom Baker), Max Martini (Agent Steve Goodrich), Val Lauren (Agent Randy Murdoch), Randle Mell (Brad Hammond), Dylan Haggerty (N.E.S.T. Tech #1), Miguel Perez (Ranger Mike Kramer), Marc Casabani (Omar), Gary Dewitt Marshall (N.E.S.T. Tech #2), Harris Yulin (Roger Stanton – uncredited)

FIELD REPORT

08:00P.M. Tony updates Jack on their progress to the airfield and says teams are already sweeping the grounds. Jack asks if they've heard from Kim, but Tony has no news for him yet. He tells Tony that they have to reach out to Kim, as she thinks she's on the run as a murder suspect. He must do whatever it takes to find her. Tony promises to continue searching for her. Kate and the hunter make their way through the woods to his home. He asks Kim why she doesn't want to go back to LA, and she tells him that it's because people think she did something she didn't do. He doesn't have a problem with that, and they arrive at his secluded home.

08:03P.M. Palmer joins Stanton's continuing interrogation and asks the NSA director if he's ready to tell them everything. Stanton doesn't reply, and Palmer asks Simmons to continue. Suddenly, Stanton begins talking – they knew about the bomb all along. Palmer asks Simmons to leave the room, and Stanton continues. The NSA had been tracking the bomb, they allowed it through customs, but there was never any danger of the bomb going off. Colonel Samuels's Coral Snake team is set to take the bomb out of play at the last possible moment. Palmer asks why they have done this, and Stanton tells him that the President's defence policy is too passive and they want to make it stronger. Palmer orders Stanton to send instructions to the Coral Snake team to take the bomb out now, but he can't. The team at Norton airfield have gone dark and will receive no further instructions until the operation is completed.

08:06P.M. The hunter, Lonnie, attempts to make Kim comfortable. He says she can shower and he'll find some clean clothes. Kim is unsure, but he assures her that the bathroom door has a lock. Tony gives Michelle the name of three more Second Wave terrorists revealed by Syed Ali during his debriefing. Mason has been given confirmation that the location of the bomb is indeed Norton airfield and orders every available field agent to attend the scene.

08:07P.M. Mason contacts Jack to brief him on the situation at the airfield. A Coral Snake team is in place, and the members will treat as hostile anybody who attempts to get to the bomb before them. Jack tells Kate that they haven't found her sister – the operation is going to take a little longer than he thought.

08:09P.M. Marie is about to leave Omar at the hangar to complete their mission – he is to fly the plane – but as she leaves, she spots the CTU team driving through the airport grounds. They have been found. On Jack's arrival at the team's secured base area, Agent Steve Goodrich hands him a dossier of personal records relating to the Coral Snake team. Jack briefs the entire team as to what they are facing, and wishes them all luck. Goodrich moves his assault team out into the field.

08:16P.M. Mason informs Tony that they are about to receive a visit from Agent Brad Hammond from Division. It's being suggested that the operation is run from the Divisional HQ, which Tony thinks would take too long to set up.

08:17P.M. Kim changes into the clothes provided by Lonnie. She examines herself in the mirror, noticing scars and bruising on her face. She joins Lonnie for dinner. As they eat, Kim tells her new friend why she can't go back to LA – the bomb. Lonnie tells her that was why he moved out to the country – because he was afraid of a terrorist strike. After they eat, he is going to show her something.

08:19P.M. Novick informs Palmer that he has found a new link to Stanton – Michigan Senator Bruce Gluck. Palmer says Sherry knew Gluck very well after their work together on the Primaries, and asks that she be brought in. Novick is shocked – bring Sherry into the OC? Lynne thinks it's a terrible idea, but Palmer indicates that the subject is not up for discussion. Agent Murdoch continues to work on the fragment of burnt paper while Michelle discusses with Tony the impending visit from Division. Tony thinks that as soon as they see the condition Mason is in, he'll be pulled from command of CTU.

08:22P.M. Jack's team locates a set of bootprints belonging to a standard issue military boot outside a building, and he leads the team inside to search. As they move through the building, Jack discovers the bodies of the Coral Snake unit, all shot through the head. Goodrich asks who's tracking the bomb if the Coral Snake team is dead?

08:28P.M. Tony and Michelle argue with Brad Hammond about the need for keeping their operation based at CTU. He disagrees with them and orders Tony to arrange for his people to start moving over to Division. Mason emerges from his office, having pulled it together enough to convince Hammond that they can handle everything from CTU.

08:30P.M. Lonnie shows Kim his big secret – a bomb shelter, deep beneath the house. As he shows her around, Kim notices guns, knives and dynamite dotted around, and suddenly realises that her kindly hunter is a Grade A whack-job. She runs from the shelter and he follows her. He asks her what is wrong, and Kim tells him she got claustrophobic. She tells him that she can't stay there and she wants to go to her Aunt Carol's.

08:34P.M. Lynne escorts Sherry to the OC, providing her with access cards. As they descend, words are exchanged. Lynne wants Sherry to run everything past her so they can maintain some kind of protocol, and Sherry accuses Lynne of positioning herself between Sherry and Palmer's inner circle. Lynne finally tells Sherry that she doesn't like her and doesn't trust her. Sherry strides out of the lift and surveys the OC with a triumphant grin on her face.

08:40P.M. As they are preparing to leave the shack, Kim and Lonnie are disturbed by the Park Ranger. Kim hides inside and Lonnie goes out to speak to him. The Ranger is searching for a girl who's wanted for kidnap and murder. Lonnie says he doesn't know anything about her, and the Ranger goes on his way. Lonnie asks Kim about the kidnap and murder and she tells him she didn't do it. He doesn't really care, and she tells him he's been a good friend.

08:42P.M. Palmer updates Sherry and tells her he wants information on any meetings with Gluck attended by both Eric Rayburn and Roger Stanton. Sherry thanks her ex-husband for letting her inside the OC. He tells her she has a job to do. Novick informs the President that Jack Bauer has located the six members of Coral Snake and that they are dead. They have yet to locate the bomb. Palmer storms into Stanton's interrogation room. He tells Stanton that all six members of the team are dead. Stanton is horrified – there were seven operatives in the Coral Snake unit.

08:45P.M. Murdoch completes his analysis of the paper and has the registration number of the plane. Michelle locates the hangar where the plane is held at Norton. Tony gives Jack the information and the CTU team moves out. The transport van that carried the bomb to the airport leaves the hangar and Marie steps back inside. She kisses Omar good luck and she opens the hangar door as he gets into the plane. With the door open, Marie leaves by the back entrance and Omar taxis the plane out as the CTU team arrives. Jack leads the chase and a roadblock is set up to cut off Omar. Climbing on to the roof of the truck, Jack fires at the wheels of the plane then shoots and wounds Omar. The plane comes to a halt and the team moves in to secure the plane. The bomb is in the back.

08:53P.M. Hammond clears CTU to continue until the crisis has ended. Lonnie scans the police band radio to see if there's anything about Kim. As he listens, he suddenly tells her that the bomb has gone off – all the stations have gone dead. Kim doesn't believe him at first until she hears the static on the radio. Lonnie convinces her to come down with him into the bunker where he seals the door.

08:55P.M. Obviously the bomb hasn't gone off and Jack is supervising the team attempting to disarm it. The bomb officer says they can't diffuse it and the timer suddenly accelerates. The officer suddenly realises that it's not actually a bomb – it's a decoy. Jack alerts the team. Palmer talks to Stanton, telling him that the bomb is not at the airport. If he has any more information that could save lives, he must tell them now. Stanton tells the President to ask Sherry. Tick tick tick...

CTU INCIDENT REPORT

Haven't I Seen You Somewhere Before?: Max Martini (Agent Steve Goodrich) is a veteran of many TV series, having appeared in *Taken*, *Breaking News* and the aborted Chris Carter series *Harsh Realm*. He also played Cpl. Henderson in *Saving Private Ryan* (1998). Randle Mell (Brad Hammond) appeared as Patrick Freeman in *Cookie's Fortune* (1998). He also appeared in *Wyatt Earp* (1994) and *The Postman* (1997).

Behind The Camera: Maurice Hurley is best known to genre fans as one of the architects of *Star Trek: The Next Generation*, although his involvement as a producer and writer were limited beyond the first season. His other television credits include writer and producer duties for *The Equaliser*, *Baywatch* and *Baywatch Nights*, *Diagnosis Murder*, and the seemingly obligatory audition piece for *24*, *La Femme Nikita*.

Time Checks: At **08:00 P.M.**, Tony updates Jack that his team is **10 minutes** away from the airfield. Mason says it will take at least **an hour and a half** to transport and set up his people at Division. At **08:40 P.M.**, Lonnie tells Kim that the highway is **15 minutes** walk away.

Fashion Police: It's just another conveyor belt of high-fashion combat fatigues this week. Yawn.

The Perils Of Kim: Is this the point where we can shake our heads in wonder? Sorry Kim, but in which universe was this guy not going to be a nutter? We all do stupid things when we're 19, sure, but Lonnie's performance at the radio was Liz Hurley bad. How could anybody, even dear, sweet, dim Kim be convinced by that? Still, she could always try putting a grenade in his coffee. On the other hand, if Elisha Cuthbert wandered into my backyard, I think I'd be tempted to lock her in the cellar too.

It's Not Easy Being Jack: Jack has quite an easy time of it this week and gets to run around being all heroic and manly. Don't you just love the way he holds a gun and torch at the same time? Thankfully, he doesn't take it too far by diving out on to the plane's wing like David Hasslehoff in *Knight Rider*. He aims carefully at the tyres and takes them out. Much more civilised.

Great Lines:

Palmer: 'You were trying to hijack my presidency?'
Stanton: 'No, but I'd like to give it some balls.'

Jack: 'Good luck, gentlemen.'

Lonnie: 'Look over the fence once in a while. The whole world hates America.'

Death Count: Six Coral Snake soldiers bring the death count up to 75. Obviously Syed Ali's budget didn't run to getting Omar his very own cyanide pellet.

DEBRIEF

An episode that's more about action than anything else. Kiefer Sutherland runs through darkened corridors with a gun as if he were born to it. Playing Jack Bauer is obviously the vocation he was destined for. Here we're seeing him very much as Jack the Leader. The team respects him, but not only is he an accomplished commander, he's still a good soldier in the field. Jack will take point and do what needs to be done. Of course, he's wearing a cool leather jacket and has a bit of stubble now and will take all the credit, but that's what being a TV star is all about.

No sign of Bob Warner this week (that guy is *still* hiding something, he must be) but things appear to be moving to a resolution on the Roger Stanton storyline as he finally dobbs in Sherry to David. It will be interesting to see just how she manages to slime her way out of that one, and did you see the look on her face when she strutted out of the lift into the OC? Like Darth Vader getting the keys to Death Star for the first time off his dad. Priceless.

Pulse-Rate: 115 bpm

Questions Arising:

- Where is the seventh member of the Coral Snake team and why did he shoot his comrades?
- Where is the bomb now?

10:00 P.M.

Production Code: 2AFF14
Written by Joel Surnow and Michael Loceff
Directed by Jon Cassar

> *'The following takes place between 9:00P.M. and 10:00P.M.... Events occur in real time.'*

Guest Starring: Reiko Aylesworth (Michelle Dessler), Jude Ciccolella (Mike Novick), Laura Harris (Marie Warner), John Terry (Bob Warner), Kevin Dillon (Lonnie McRae), Max Martini (Agent Steve Goodrich), Lourdes Benedicto (Carrie Turner), Daniel Dae Kim (Agent Tom Baker), Dylan Haggerty (N.E.S.T. Tech #1), Michael Mantell (Steve Hillenburg), Marc Casabani (Omar), Adam Vernier (Gus), Zina Zaflow (Melinda)

FIELD REPORT

09:00P.M. The CTU forces continue to search as Jack asks Omar where the real bomb is. He doesn't answer, and Jack requests the presence of a translator. At CTU, Mason is beginning to deteriorate, pulling clumps of hair from his scalp. Jack calls him to request that they use time-lapse satellite images to trace the plane back to its original position. That's where the real bomb will have been swapped over. Jack is concerned that Mason is no longer fit for duty and should think about passing on command to Tony. Mason assures Jack that he can handle it, then briefs him on the seventh Coral Snake operative. It seems likely that he murdered his comrades. It appears that Omar wants to talk, but the translator has not arrived yet. Kate speaks to her father for the first time. As they talk, Jack asks for her to come and help with the translation. Kate tells her father that she loves him. Palmer confronts Sherry with the information that Roger Stanton gave him. He also informs her that the bomb is missing. She is horrified and begins talking. She was contacted by somebody high up in the NSA several months previously, requesting that she help in advising where her husband's weaknesses lay. She assures Palmer that she was doing this to help him, not bring him down, and asks for time to be able to prove that she's not lying.

09:09P.M. Kate attempts to translate as Omar is interrogated. He tells her he was doing this for his family. Kate runs into difficulties as she speaks a different dialect, but the translator arrives to take over. Jack thanks Kate for her help as the translator asks Omar about the second bomb. He claims he doesn't know anything. Jack steps forward and looks down on the terrorist menacingly.

09:10P.M. As Kate is led back to the secured area, she thinks she spots a disguised Marie attempting to leave the airport among the civilians. She goes to investigate.

09:15P.M. Kim and Lonnie sit inside the bunker. Kim wants to get in touch with her dad, but Lonnie says they have to stay down in the bunker as they don't know which way the radiation cloud will travel. He goes to try the short-wave radio and pulls a connection from the back so Kim won't hear anything. He tells her he can't pick up anything, and attempts to comfort the frightened Kim.

09:17 P.M. Mason greets Paula's replacement, Carrie Turner. As they talk, he begins to cough violently. Carrie asks him who she should report to, and Mason tells her to report to him. Carrie, without wanting to cause offence, tells him that rumours are flying that he won't be around for much longer, and Mason says she can report to Tony and Michelle. At the mention of Michelle Dessler's name, Carrie bristles – she used to be Michelle's boss at Division. As they talk, Mason collapses.

At the airfield, Kate looks through the lines of civilians filing through security checks before they leave. She thinks she spots Marie disappearing into the back of the hangar and tries to follow, but is stopped by a security officer. She shows him her CTU ID tag, and the officer lets her through. Kate asks him to contact Jack Bauer to tell him that Marie Warner is here. As Kate moves through the back of the darkened hangar, Marie surprises her, holding her sister at gunpoint. Kate asks what has happened to her, and Marie replies that she opened her eyes. Marie demands Kate's ID badge so she can escape, and throws her to the ground. Just as Marie is about to pull the trigger and kill another loved one, she is shot in the arm and falls to the ground, screaming in pain. Jack and a team arrived just in time.

09:27 P.M. Marie is dragged screaming into the secured area to be interrogated. Kate begs Jack to give her sister something for the pain. Jack refuses – he'll give her something after she tells them where the bomb is. Kate has to let him do this his way. Jack talks to Marie. He tells her she's in so much pain because the bullet is still lodged in her arm. As soon as she tells him where the bomb is, he'll give her something for the pain. Marie tells him she's not afraid to die.

09:31 P.M. Things are a little tense back at *chez* bunker, and Lonnie goes to check the radio again. Kim asks if there's any sugar for the coffee, and Lonnie points her to the back. While retrieving the sugar, Kim finds a TV, and as Lonnie is distracted with the radio, she switches it on – to discover that every channel is broadcasting as normal. Michelle and Tony turn up the ID of the missing Coral Snake operative – Captain Jonathan Wallace. Tony heads off and Carrie pops over to say hi to Michelle. Michelle isn't happy to see her.

09:34 P.M. Mason speaks to Tony and informs him that he is stepping down as Director of CTU. He hands Tony his access codes, but Tony says he can't take them – the new Director should have them. Mason tells Tony he is the new Director of CTU, and walks out of the building.

09:40 P.M. Tony announces to the assembled staff of CTU that Mason has taken his leave and he is now the new Director.

09:41 P.M. Marie starts going into shock as Jack continues the interrogation. He asks for Demerol to numb the pain for a few minutes, and asks Kate to join him to try to bring Marie back to reality. Kate coaxes her sister back to lucidity, but Marie refuses to tell her anything and the painkillers begin to wear off. As she cries in pain again, Jack tells her she'll get more drugs when she has revealed the location of the bomb. Marie eventually tells him that the bomb is in a van downtown and they have three hours before it goes off. Jack is suddenly suspicious – Marie wants his team out of the airport all of a sudden. He plays a hunch that the bomb is still at the airport, and orders a grid search of every building. As Jack rushes off, Marie mumbles that they won't find it and they're all going to die.

09:51 P.M. Palmer and Sherry speak to Steve Hillenberg, a CIA operative whom Sherry asked to be her independent source to prove that she wasn't acting against her husband. Hillenberg confirms that they have been building a case against Roger Stanton for four months. Palmer tells Sherry that she may or may not be telling the truth, but he doesn't have time to work out which it is. He has no choice but to remove her from the OC. Secret Service agents escort her from the complex.

09:55P.M. Lonnie begins making up beds for himself and Kim. She asks him for an aspirin, and when he turns his back, she slams him with a metal bar and grabs a knife. Lonnie grabs the knife off her easily, and Kim asks to be let out. He wants her to stay, as all he wanted was some company, but Kim doesn't want to. He agrees to let her go and gives her a loaded gun to scare off the cougars in the forest. As she walks up the steps he asks if she'll come back and see him. Kim tells him she doesn't think so.

09:58P.M. Jack arrives at the scene of a firefight to see one hostile going down in a hail of bullets. He was protecting a delivery truck. The team opens the back of the van and finds the bomb. Tick tick tick...

CTU INCIDENT REPORT

Haven't I Seen You Somewhere Before?: Lourdes Benedicto (Carrie Turner) has had recurring roles in *NYPD Blue*, *ER* and *Titans* and played Karen Torres in *Dawson's Creek*. Michael Mantell (Steve Hillenburg) was most recently seen in 2002's *Secretary* and also played Dr Frazier in *A.I. Artificial Intelligence*.

Time Checks: Sherry asks Palmer for **30 minutes** to prove that she's telling the truth. Jack asks for a dose of Demerol to last **five minutes**. Marie lies about the time the bomb has before it detonates – **three hours**. Sherry became involved in the plot against her husband **four months** prior to the events of today.

Fashion Police: Carrie's nicely cut suit has 'Bitch' written all over it. Look at those shoulder pads – Alexis Carrington would be proud.

The Perils Of Kim: The Adventures of Kimberley, Queen of the Wilderness continue this week, as Kim enjoys an underground adventure with her new friend Lonnie. In retrospect, looking back over the last 14 weeks, there's something quite comforting about the scrapes Kim manages to find herself in. As her dad deals with twists galore, it's become clear that we need the constancy of Kim to keep us grounded. There's also a lot to be learnt from her exploits. Like that bit at the end of *He-Man* when a character always came on to tell us the moral of this week's tale. This week, as Kim walks out on Lonnie's little hidey-hole: 'Sooner or later, we're all going to be dumped by a girl like that.'

It's Not Easy Being Jack: Jack seems out of his depth this week. It's one thing to beat up on a scumbag terrorist like Syed Ali, but Marie is a little Barbie doll and would break if Jack so much as looked at her. All credit to Jack for using his brains and getting Kate to talk to the little brat. Curiously though, when the bomb is discovered, Jack looks a little downbeat. Hang on, it's what you were looking for, you idiot! Be happy.

Great Lines:

Kate: 'Wake up Marie! You're about to become the biggest murderer in the history of this country.'

Marie: 'Nobody's innocent in this country. I'm not afraid to die.'

Jack: 'I don't believe you. I've seen people who are willing to die. I've looked them straight in the eye, just like I am you right now. You're not one of them.'

Death Count: Just one hostile protecting the bomb this week. The death count currently stands at 76, although if you look closely, you could see a bloke with a black cape and scythe following George Mason out of CTU.

DEBRIEF

Not the greatest episode of the show to date. It seems the team were treading water a little this week, getting their strength back for a big push on the last nine episodes of the season. Surprisingly, considering the build-up to finding the bomb has been ongoing for 14 weeks, its discovery seems something of an anti-climax, and brings the question into play: where do we go from here? Are we going to have a situation akin to last year where our assassin is defeated by Jack, only for it to be revealed that a second killer had already left Europe that morning? Is Jack going to disarm the bomb, then receive a call from Tony along the lines of 'Uh, Jack, you're not gonna believe this, but…'? Obviously, last year's structure problems were caused by a late commission for the second half of the season. This year the commission was for a full 24 episodes, so whatever has been planned for the remaining weeks, it should be one hell of a ride.

Other interesting points this week surround lovely, sweet Michelle Dessler, who, with the arrival of Carrie, would seem to have some skeletons in the cupboard hung alongside those purple blouses. As Sherry Palmer is escorted from the series, never fear, a new bitch has come take her place. Carrie is decked out in a business suit that's made for fighting – either she's Michelle's spurned lesbian lover, or they're both going to be revealed as Nina Myers's long lost sisters and she missed the family reunion. Special praise must go to Laura Harris who gives a cracking performance as Marie, going from calm terrorist to whiny brat within seconds. Excellent stuff.

Pulse-Rate: 110 bpm

Questions Arising:

- What is the deal between Michelle and Carrie?
- Have we seen the last of George Mason?
- Is Sherry Palmer telling the truth?

10:00 P.M. – 11:00 P.M.

Production Code: 2AFF15
Written by Robert Cochran
Directed by Ian Toynton

> *'The following takes place between 10:00P.M. and 11:00P.M.... Events occur in real time.'*

Guest Starring: Reiko Aylesworth (Michelle Dessler), Jude Ciccolella (Mike Novick), Michelle Forbes (Lynne Kresge), Max Martini (Agent Steve Goodrich), Lourdes Benedicto (Carrie Turner), Donnie Keshawarz (Yusuf Auda), Daniel Dae Kim (Agent Tom Baker), Dylan Haggerty (N.E.S.T. Tech #1), Dean Norris (General Bowden), Neal Matarazzo (Agent Graves), Susan Gibney (Female Driver), James Oliver (Male Driver), Gary Dewitt Marshall (N.E.S.T. Tech #2)

FIELD REPORT

10:00P.M. Jack has the bomb moved to a nearby hangar to allow the N.E.S.T. team to work on the device. As they work, Mason arrives. Jack asks him what he's doing there, and Mason tells him he wants to see the thing that's going to kill him laid to rest. Jack thinks he should be somewhere else, but Mason is adamant. The N.E.S.T. team is having problems with the bomb – a N.E.S.T. officer informs Jack that the trigger is tamper proof. If it's interfered with or removed from the casing, the bomb will detonate instantly. There is no way to disarm it. Jack speaks to Goodrich, briefing him that they're going to have to fly the device out of there. The airport doesn't accommodate jet planes, but Goodrich arranges to have the fastest, most reliable plane prepped. Jack puts a call in to President Palmer. As he waits, Jack asks a N.E.S.T. officer if they have a timer reading yet. The bomb will detonate in 55 minutes.

10:05P.M. Kim emerges from the woods on to the highway. As she walks up the road, a car pulls up and a guy asks if she wants a ride. At first she says yes, but as the guy tidies the passenger seat for her to sit, she has second thoughts. The guy becomes insistent, and gets out of the car. Kim pulls the gun given to her by Lonnie and tells him to get back in the car. He doesn't think she can use it, but Kim puts him right by shooting out a window. The guy jumps back in the car, shouting 'Bitch!' out of the window as he goes. Jack speaks to the President, who asks him to prepare for the two possibilities they have discussed. Palmer is about to assemble his staff and discuss their options.

10:07P.M. Novick and Lynne brief the President on the two options available to them. Novick discusses the possibility of dropping the bomb into the Pacific Ocean, 80 miles offshore. The ocean would absorb much of the radiation, but a percentage of fallout would blow back over LA. It would also wipe out a great deal of the local ecology, leading to economic and long-term health issues. Lynne outlines a plan to drop the bomb at a designated 'ground zero' in the Mojave Desert, from where no resources are taken.

Fallout would be minimal. This is the agreed plan, but to assure accuracy, whoever flew the plane would have to go down with it. Palmer calls Jack to notify him of their findings, and Jack says CTU has come to the same conclusion. Jack indicates that they have a number of volunteers for the mission.

10:11 P.M. Mason overheard Jack's conversation with Palmer, and asks Jack where the volunteers are. He knows that Jack is going to fly the plane himself – Jack says he is a proficient enough pilot to get the plane in the air and put it down. Mason volunteers but Jack refuses, as he doesn't think he's capable of getting the plane where they need it. Jack orders the bomb to be loaded on to the plane.

10:17 P.M. Tony greets Agent Graves, who is bringing items found at Syed Ali's safe house in for examination. He is also introduced to Yusuf Auda, the intelligence liaison from the Middle Eastern government who assisted with finding Ali's safe house. Auda is keen to help, but Tony attempts to keep him out of the loop. He asks Michelle to keep an eye on Auda and for him not to be shown anything they don't want him to see. Graves gives Tony a hard drive from Ali's possessions that they haven't been able to access yet.

10:19 P.M. As the bomb is loaded, Jack speaks to Tony, saying that he is flying the plane and wants to speak to Kim while he still has time. Tony gets on to it. Kim is still walking, but manages to get a lift from a passing woman. She asks the woman if she can call her father.

10:22 P.M. Jack climbs aboard the plane. Kate watches, horrified, as he taxis down the runway and takes off.

10:28 P.M. Novick informs the President of the plane's progress. Palmer asks that Air Force One be readied for take-off as soon as possible. He wants to go to Los Angeles. Novick and Lynne think this is a bad idea and attempt to dissuade him. Once the bomb goes off, Palmer wants to reassure the public. Lynne makes the arrangements. Palmer is shocked to discover that Jack Bauer is flying the plane.

10:31 P.M. Tony patches through to Jack aboard the plane – he has Kim on the other line. Father and daughter share a tearful farewell. Jack tells her how much he loves her, and Kim apologises for being so horrible to him. Jack says goodbye.

10:39 P.M. The woman pulls over and asks Kim what she wants to do. Kim wants to be alone and runs from the car. Michelle comes to Tony with information taken from the hard drive. They found the recording of a conversation between Syed Ali and high-ranking government officials from three Middle Eastern countries. It seems these countries bought the bomb and supplied it to Ali. Tony puts a call in to the President. He informs Palmer of what they have discovered and that they are verifying the authenticity of the recordings. Palmer briefs Novick on this new situation. If the evidence shows three Middle Eastern powers to be behind the bomb, they could be at war very soon.

10:43 P.M. Aboard the plane, Jack sets the autopilot on to the final line of approach. As he sits back, he hears a noise behind him and turns round, pulling his gun on… George Mason. Jack is not happy to see him, even less so when Mason shows him the parachute he's brought along. He *will* take the plane down. Mason wonders if Jack has a death wish and if this isn't the easy way out. Leave all your troubles behind and go down as one of the greatest heroes the country has ever seen. Mason tells him to go out and pull the pieces of his life back together, assuring Jack that he can do this. Jack finally agrees, thanking Mason.

10:52 P.M. Jack is going to bail out at the last possible minute. He patches through to CTU and requests a chopper in the air immediately to trail the plane and pick him up. Tony is aghast that Mason is taking the plane in, but asks Michelle to take care of Jack's request. Auda asks Tony what they have discovered on the hard drive, but Tony informs the intelligence liaison that he doesn't have the necessary clearance to be told that. Auda is not happy, as his country has acted in good faith.

10:54 P.M. Palmer speaks with General Bowden, who wishes to discuss retaliation against the Middle Eastern powers. Palmer points out that they do not have positive proof yet, but the Joint Chiefs wish to proceed for the time being as if they have – they want to activate plans to invade the countries in question. Palmer is cautious, but asks for them to proceed. He tells Lynne: 'We may be talking about World War Three.' Aboard the plane, Jack prepares to bail out. Mason asks Jack to look in on his son from time to time. Jack promises that he will. The pair say goodbye and Jack jumps from the plane.

10:57 P.M. Novick tells the President that he will be able to see the explosion on the eastern horizon. Solemnly, Palmer takes his seat to wait. With 90 seconds remaining, Mason powers the plane into its final dive. Jack ignites a flare to light his descent on to the desert floor. On landing, he rushes for cover behind a rock face and counts down the remaining seconds. The bomb detonates. Kim sees the blast and believes her father has just died. Palmer watches the explosion from Air Force One – has World War III just begun? Jack watches the mushroom cloud blossom over the desert. RIP George Mason. Tick tick tick…

CTU INCIDENT REPORT

Haven't I Seen You Somewhere Before?: Dean Norris (General Bowden) seems to have made a career out of playing SWAT team leaders, appearing in both *Gremlins 2: The New Batch* (1990) and *Terminator 2: Judgement Day.* He was also a regular in the short-lived TV spin off from the film series *Tremors.* Susan Gibney (Female Driver) had the honour of playing the designer of the USS *Enterprise* in several episodes of *Star Trek: The Next Generation,* and, like *24* guest star before her Steven Culp (Agent Simmons), ended up on the cutting room floor in *Star Trek: Nemesis.* She also appeared as a lab tech in the pilot episode of *CSI:*

Crime Scene Investigation, her character having been on a disastrous date with Grissom.

Behind The Camera: British director Ian Toynton began his career working on some of the best British television of the seventies. He was a dubbing editor on the pilot episode of *The Sweeney* and would go on to edit episodes of the series proper and the second of *The Sweeney* movies. He has directed episodes of *Minder*, *Bergerac*, *Widows* and *CATS Eyes*. In America he has directed episodes of *JAG*, *The Cape*, *Profiler*, *The Pretender*, *Relic Hunter*, for which he also wrote an episode, and segments of the crime drama *Crossing Jordan*.

Time Checks: Jack asks for a reading on the bomb timer and is told it will detonate in **55 minutes**. Is there a possibility that there may also be 55 minutes remaining until the end of the episode? Mason must put the plane into a dive with **1:30** remaining on the clock. Jack bails out of the plane **four minutes** before impact.

Fashion Police: Yusuf Auda is nicely turned out in a natty jacket that Jack would approve of. These two should get on very well in coming episodes. And really, Tony, you could be a bit more polite, he's the kind of lad you could take home to meet your mother.

The Perils Of Kim: There is absolutely nothing that can be said against Kim is this episode. She shows that she's her father's daughter when she pulls the gun on the jerk in the car. You can just see Jack smiling and growling, 'That's my girl!' When it comes down to the crunch, there should not have been a dry eye in the house when the poor lass is speaking to her superhero dad – if there was, we'll be sending the boys round to have a word. Don't you just want to give her a hug? The moral of this week's story is: 'Sometimes, you've just got to give a girl a break.'

It's Not Easy Being Jack: It was obviously time for Jack and George to get in touch with their inner woman. Who'd have thought that from Jack shooting his former boss with a tranq dart way back in the pilot episode, we'd get to them saying goodbye to each other like this? Of course, Jack had to be in there first with taking the bomb down – the weight of the world on your shoulders can only get heavier with time. Although he could have been well aware that Mason would pull a stowaway stunt and was just doing it to look hot in front of Kate, knowing that he'd be getting a taxi home from the desert in half an hour.

Great Lines:

Jack: 'Honey, I want you to live your life. I want you to be happy, that's all I've ever wanted for you. I want you to try and grow up and be the kind of person that would have made your mom proud. Promise me that.'

Mason (to Jack): 'The service is bad enough on this flight, you don't have to shoot me.'

Mason (to Jack): 'You wanna be a real hero? Here's what you do. You get back down there and you put the pieces together. Find a way to forgive yourself for what happened to your wife. You make things right with your daughter and you go on serving your country. And it takes some real guts.'

Death Count: The award for most selfless sacrifice in a TV drama has to go to George Mason, who brings the totaliser up to a healthy 77. Of course, we're not counting assorted hermits, campers, hikers and the occasional prairie dog who might have been sitting on top of the blast, so let's not quibble.

DEBRIEF

A truly superb episode on every level that has you gripped from the moment that clock starts ticking. Of course, it was no surprise that Mason would save the day and go out in a blaze of glory, but nevertheless, this was edge of the seat. All credit to Xander Berkley for turning George Mason from a pen-pushing imbecile into the one character on the show who we truly care about. There was never any front with George, and we always knew where we stood (a feat in itself on *24*). He's had the best lines and will be missed for the last nine episodes. We salute you, sir.

Of course, with the imminent break-out of World War III, it ain't over till the fat lady sings. Bring it on!

Pulse-Rate: 130 bpm

Questions Arising:

- Is the recording genuine?
- Is Yusuf Auda working for or against America?
- Is the world about to be screwed with its pants on?

11:00 P.M.
12:00 A.M.

Production Code: 2AFF16
Written by Howard Gordon and Evan Katz
Directed by Ian Toynton

> *'The following takes place between 11:00P.M. and 12:00A.M.... Events occur in real time.'*

Guest Starring: Reiko Aylesworth (Michelle Dessler), Jude Ciccolella (Mike Novick), Michelle Forbes (Lynne Kresge), Lourdes Benedicto (Carrie Turner), Gregg Henry (Jonathan Wallace), Francesco Quinn (Syed Ali), Donnie Keshawarz (Yusuf Auda), Lombardo Boyar (Ramon Garcia), Dean Norris (General Bowden), Daniel Dae Kim (Agent Tom Baker), Christopher Maher (Deputy Prime Minister)

FIELD REPORT

11:00P.M. At CTU, staff watch the explosion on a satellite monitor screen. On-board Air Force One, President Palmer watches solemnly as the explosion lights up the horizon. In the wilderness, Kim watches with tears on her face, believing she is all alone now. In the desert Jack lights flares to signal to the approaching CTU chopper. He climbs aboard for the journey back to LA.

11:05P.M. Tony speaks to the staff of CTU. On behalf of the late George, he thanks them all for their help in getting to where they are, but they still have work to do. The recording taken in Cyprus is of top priority as it is central to any military response being planned by Washington. Yusuf Auda accuses Tony of deliberately excluding him from the investigation. Tony continues to be unco-operative in this matter, and Auda storms off. Carrie joins Tony as they head for a meeting to discuss the authenticity of the recordings. Michelle won't be joining them as she is interrogating Ali. Michelle questions Ali about the recording, and he refuses to talk, but eventually he tells Michelle he will say whatever she wants him to say. She wants the truth, and Ali claims he has never spoken to any of the men on the recording. He claims he was in Berlin on the date the meeting supposedly took place. The bomb was a Second Wave operation only.

11:09P.M. Tony and Carrie meet with the audio experts who have analysed the recording. They believe it to be an accurate recording of a meeting that took place between four men who were conspiring to detonate a nuclear bomb on US soil; it hasn't been faked. Michelle joins the meeting, informing Tony that Ali maintains the recording has been faked. She feels he could be telling the truth. Tony wonders if he's trying to save the rest of his family – Ali still believes that they killed his eldest son – but Michelle thinks that if there's even the remotest possibility he's telling the truth they have to check it out. Carrie counters this, feeling that the word of an attempted mass murderer is not to be trusted, and, with due respect, Michelle is not the most experienced interrogator. Tony picks up on tension between Michelle and Carrie, and says that they're finished.

11:12P.M. On-board Air Force One, Novick briefs Palmer on the co-ordinates of the explosion – within a few metres of the designated site. Palmer wishes to pass on his personal condolences to Kimberley Bauer, but Novick tells him that Jack wasn't on the plane after all. Lynne informs Palmer that CTU believes the Cyprus recording to be genuine. She passes round transcripts, which show the Middle Eastern ministers giving direct support to Ali's cause. Palmer asks for the Joint Chiefs to be assembled and also for the Hill to be notified of an emergency session, during which he will be asking for a formal declaration of war.

11:18P.M. Tony speaks to Michelle about her report for the Pentagon on the interrogation of Ali. She asks for more time. Tony asks her if she's OK after her run-in with Carrie, and she tells him she's tired. He apologises for putting Michelle in that position, but she says they have to follow up any possibility. There is definite tension in the air between them. On-board Air Force One, Palmer is in discussions with General Bowden and the Joint Chiefs. It will take eight to ten weeks to have the military in a go position, but they are ready for a rolling start with surgical bombing operations that will weaken the enemy military. The planes can be airborne by the time Palmer speaks to the country the following morning. Lynne informs the President that the Deputy Prime Minister of one of the Middle Eastern powers is on the line for the second time. Palmer doesn't want to talk to him – they are making plans to invade his country after all. Novick and Lynne believe they should speak to avoid any suspicion. The Deputy Prime Minister is put through. He offers solidarity to America and assistance with prosecuting Syed Ali. He also urges Palmer not to make any rash political decisions.

11:22P.M. Syed Ali is being transferred from CTU as Jack arrives back. Tony gives Jack the name of a police officer who should be able to help him locate Kim.

11:23P.M. Jack calls the police officer, but can't get through. Michelle speaks to Jack about Ali and how she thinks he's telling the truth about the Cyprus recording. Michelle asks Jack if he'll speak to Ali, but Jack is more concerned with finding Kim. Eventually he agrees to speak with Ali and asks Michelle to keep trying the police officer. Carrie has been watching the pair speak.

11:25P.M. As Ali is led from the CTU building under high security, Jack catches up with him. He tells Ali that they faked the death of his son, and asks if the Cyprus recording is a fake. Ali maintains that what he told Michelle is true. Jack thanks him and as he moves away, Ali is shot in the head by a sniper's bullet.

11:31P.M. Tony discusses Ali's death with Jack. Who could have known they were having Ali moved? Jack points out that half the intelligence community would have known about the transfer. Tony believes that one of the countries implicated on the Cyprus recording must be behind the assassination, but Jack disagrees. In light of this, he's inclined to believe that Ali told the truth, and Jack tells Tony he has a responsibility to look into this properly. Tony grows hostile at this, thanks Jack for his help and tells him to go and find his daughter.

11:34P.M. Kim arrives at a convenience store in the middle of nowhere. It is closed, and when she tries the payphone, all services are busy. The manager of the store comes out and she asks to use the bathroom. As Kim heads into the back, the manager locks the main doors. The President is still in discussions with the military, planning their next course of action. Bowden estimates that there will be 10–30,000 US casualties in the coming war. If Russia and China weigh in against the U.S., there will be even more.

11:35P.M. Jack contacts the President, who breaks off from the meeting to speak to him. Jack informs him about Ali's assassination and his belief that the terrorist may have been telling the truth. He thinks that the President may be being coerced into making the wrong military decision. Palmer tells him he can't change their operation based on conjecture, and he'll need proof. Jack doesn't have much time to find it.

11:41 P.M. Jack speaks to Michelle over the phone and briefs her on his conversation with Palmer. They need to find proof – one of the foreign intelligence agencies must have been tracking Ali's movements. Michelle tells Jack about the presence of Yusuf Auda. Jack will run a background check on him. Kate is led into CTU for her debriefing, spotting Jack as he works. She is surprised to see him and he tells her it's a long story. Baker leads her away for her debrief.

11:43 P.M. Novick informs the President of the good news that the Joint Chiefs have revised down their casualty estimate. Palmer is bothered by his conversation with Bauer – he's worried that they may be moving too fast. Novick cautions him – they have verified evidence and they must act on it. Palmer doesn't want to make a mistake just to satisfy the public's bloodlust. Jack attempts to speak to Auda. He wants to ask him about the evidence, but Auda refuses to talk unless Jack gives him information in return – evidence Jack is unable to give. Auda tells him he is asking too much and walks away. Jack receives a call on his mobile. The unknown caller tells him he killed Syed Ali and can give Jack the evidence he needs as he planted the Cyprus recording. All he wants in return is Kate Warner and Jack has to bring her to a meeting point.

11:52 P.M. As Kim uses the bathroom, she hears a commotion outside. A man is asking the manager to open the store – he needs supplies as he is heading into the mountains with his pregnant wife. The man begins to grow violent and the manager calls the police. As he does so, the man smashes the window and enters the store, attacking the manager. Kim pulls her gun and fires a warning shot, but the man advances on her and takes the gun. He starts filling a trolley with supplies.

11:55 P.M. Jack contacts Michelle. He tells her Auda still has some trust issues, but there may be another way to find what they need. He'll need her help. At the store, the man offers to pay for what he's taking, but Kim tells him to go. He pulls the gun, screaming that he wants to pay and the manager goes to the cash register. He turns the TV on, and they see a news report about the explosion. The police pull up outside and as the man is distracted, the manager attempts to get the gun. He is shot in the struggle. Panicking, the man grabs Kim.

11:57 P.M. Michelle distracts Agent Baker from his debrief with Kate, which gives Jack chance to move her. They make their way through the main CTU office, observed by both Auda and Carrie. Carrie informs Tony that she thinks Jack is taking Kate from the building. Tony cuts off their route, holding Jack at gunpoint. Jack disarms him, Tony's ankle twisting beneath him as he goes down. Jack and Kate make their way to the parking lot. Tick tick tick...

CTU INCIDENT REPORT

Haven't I Seen You Somewhere Before?: Lombardo Boyar (Ramon Garcia) appeared in *Gone In Sixty Seconds* (2000) and has a semi-regular role in *The Bernie Mac Show*.

Time Checks: At **11:18 P.M.**, Michelle requests another **15 minutes** to prepare her report for the Pentagon. Palmer is scheduled to go on the air in **six hours**. The caller gives Jack **30 minutes** to bring Kate Warner to him.

Fashion Police: With a lack of major new characters, we've had no fashion suspects since Carrie Turner arrived with that suit. It's a good guess that we haven't seen Bob Warner for a few weeks as they're giving John Terry's beard a chance to grow back.

The Perils Of Kim: Only Kim could get herself into a hostage situation minutes after losing her dad. Frying pan/fire, rock/hard place (delete as applicable). Is there a moral this week?

'When people are kicking the crap out of each other, sometimes it's best just to let them get on with it.'

It's Not Easy Being Jack: Do you ever have one of those days when you just can't get out of the office? You'd think after saving LA from a nuclear bomb Jack'd be able to go and take Kim for ice cream, but no. Now he's expected to save the entire world from nuclear Armageddon. Sigh. And, where the hell does Tony get off on lecturing Jack about how he does his job? The fact that Jack doesn't sniffily tell him, 'Yeah, well you need to stop sleeping with co-workers who turn out to be international terrorists who sell secrets', just shows how polite he is. Whilst Tony's skulking around the subdued lighting of CTU staring moodily over computer monitors at Michelle, at least Jack's out in the field firing guns and getting to do cool stuff.

Great Lines:

Tony: 'Don't lecture me on responsibility, Jack. Come on, we both know how you work. You consider going against the grain as some kind of a virtue.'

Death Count: At least Syed Ali got to hear that his son was still alive before getting a bullet between his eyes. Death count currently stands at 78.

Trivia: The scenes set on-board Air Force One appear to have been shot on the same set as used by *The West Wing*. This is the same standing set that was originally constructed for use in the film *Air Force One* (1997) which featured Xander Berkeley.

DEBRIEF

A slightly snoozeworthy episode on the whole, which comes as a disappointment after the dramatic build-up of last week's episode.

There aren't many surprises here – Ali's death was really on the cards from the moment of his capture, as was the fact that Palmer appears to be still being coerced into heading towards full scale war. With Stanton and Sherry out of the picture, the possibilities are greatly reduced, with both Lynne and Novick in the frame. If there was money on this, Mike Novick would be coming in at 2-1, but with the way we were sucker-punched with Marie, it's still anybody's race.

The lacklustre feel of this hour does question the wisdom of having the bomb going off with nine episodes to go. How far can you take audience expectation and energy before they give up? Somehow, the threat of World War III appears less immediate and gripping than the danger of a single nuclear device on your doorstep. Can the boys bring the energy back up to the boil in the next eight weeks?

Pulse-Rate: 100 bpm

Questions Arising:

? Who is the mysterious caller?

? Why does he need Kate?

12:00 A.M.

1:00 A.M.

Production Code: 2AFF17
Written by Evan Katz and Gil Grant
Directed by Jon Cassar

> ***'The following takes place between 12:00A.M. and 1:00A.M.… Events occur in real time.'***

Guest Starring: Reiko Aylesworth (Michelle Dessler), Jude Ciccolella (Mike Novick), Michelle Forbes (Lynne Kresge), Lourdes Benedicto (Carrie Turner), Gregg Henry (Jonathan Wallace), Donnie Keshawarz (Yusuf Auda), Alan Dale (Vice President Prescott), Sterling Macer Jr (Deputy Raynes), Justin Louis (Danny), Lombardo Boyar (Ramon Garcia), Jamison Jones (Deputy Nirman), Nicole Gomez Fisher (Mrs Garcia), Shontina Vernon (Agent Zoltan), Doc Duhame (Man with Gun)

FIELD REPORT

12:00A.M. As Jack and Kate make their way to the parking lot, Carrie finds the injured Tony. She requests a medic and phones through to security to have Jack stopped at the gate. Kate asks Jack to explain before she goes anywhere with him, but they don't have time, he'll explain in the car. They manage to get through security just as Carrie phones through. As Jack drives, he explains to Kate that he received a call from a man who says he has evidence that can prove the Cyprus recording is a fake and avert the impending war. He wouldn't give Jack anything until he brought Kate to him. He asks Kate if she's prepared to take the risk and help her country. A medic attends to Tony as Carrie tells him Jack got away. She also thinks that Michelle was helping Jack – she spotted her taking Baker away from Kate's debrief minutes before she found Tony.

12:05A.M. Palmer has landed in Los Angeles. En route in his car, he takes a call from the Vice President, who is requesting authority to inform the British Ambassador of their response to the bomb. Palmer refuses on the grounds that it's a little premature, and briefs the Vice President on the possibility that the tape may be a fake. The Vice President is keen to proceed and tells Palmer it's a little late for second thoughts. Both Novick and Lynne register their discomfort with Palmer's faith in Jack Bauer and the falseness of the recording. He notes their comments. The police have surrounded the convenience store as Kim attempts to keep the manager alive. Garcia is crying – he didn't mean for this to happen. He was only trying to protect his pregnant wife, as there's a war coming. Kim urges him to give himself up, but he doesn't respond. The store manager goes into arrest.

12:09A.M. Jack notices that they are being followed and pulls into a side alley. A few seconds later, a car pulls in after them. Jack emerges with his gun drawn as Kate pulls the SUV across the alley to block the escape. It is Yusuf. He followed Jack as nobody is giving out information. He saw Jack take out Tony, and knows he is not on-board with what CTU is doing. He feels his country is being implicated in the bomb, but he argues that his country would not ally itself with an attack that will decimate it. He knows that Jack is now isolated and wants to help. At CTU, Tony asks Michelle if she deliberately lured Agent Baker away so Jack could get Kate Warner out of the building. She lies and wonders if Carrie told him that. She believes Carrie wants her out of CTU because she knows that Michelle doesn't like her. She doesn't want to talk about it.

12:17A.M. Kim tells Garcia that she'll tell the police it was an accident, but he thinks he's going to prison for life. The police phone the store and Garcia speaks to them. They put his wife on, and he tells her that he's killed a man. He asks that his wife is taken to her sister's in Monta Ray, and when she's there, he'll release Kim.

12:19A.M. Jack and Kate arrive at the warehouse. As Jack tools up with guns from the back of the SUV, he tells Kate to stay in the car while he goes in. She can contact his mobile if she gets into trouble. Jack heads inside the warehouse, finding the man inside. He orders the man to drop his weapon, and he complies. He is Captain Jonathan Wallace, the seventh member of the Coral Snake unit. His unit were responsible for ensuring the bomb went off and planting the Cyprus recording to start a war. The men he is acting for control oil, and their holdings would quadruple for years in the event of a Middle Eastern war. He needs Kate Warner to arrange transport for him out of the country through the family company, as the men who hired him are now attempting to have him killed. In return, he'll give Jack evidence against the Cyprus recording. As he talks, Wallace is able to signal to his man on the outside.

12:23A.M. Kate waits for Jack in the SUV. Wallace's associate creeps up and orders her out of the vehicle at gunpoint. Kate is saved by Auda, who knocks the man unconscious. Jack asks Wallace how the evidence will discredit the Cyprus recording. Wallace has the original tapes before they were mixed down into the fake recording. Auda contacts Jack to tell him he's taken care of Wallace's associate and he'll be out for a while. Wallace is still refusing to give up anything without Kate. An unscheduled charter can only be arranged if a Warner Company partner is on-board, and with Bob Warner in custody that leaves Kate. Naturally, she'll be eliminated afterwards. Jack cannot let that happen, and Wallace gets up to leave. As he goes, Jack realises he has no choice and asks Auda to bring Kate in.

12:31A.M. District Headquarters, Los Angeles Palmer has set up at the District HQ. Novick tells Lynne that he needs to speak to Jack Bauer. The President is basing a lot on one conversation with the CTU agent, and feels that if he spoke to Bauer he would be less in the dark and more able to guide the President. Lynne is unhappy that he's doing this behind Palmer's back, which he notes, and Lynne finally gives him the CTU number. Tony takes the call from Novick, and informs Novick that they are attempting to locate Jack themselves. Novick asks that as soon as they make contact, Jack should be put through to him.

12:33A.M. Tony asks Carrie to join him in his office. He asks her to put a filter on Michelle's phone and e-mails so they can monitor her actions and find out when Jack attempts contact.

12:35A.M. Mrs Garcia is helped into a squad car and driven away. Garcia accuses Kim of getting him into this mess because she pointed her gun at him. He blames her for ruining his life. She tells him she was afraid, and he screams at her, asking what she has to be afraid of. She says her dad died tonight in the explosion, which seems to appease Garcia a little. The phone rings again – the police are informing Garcia that his wife is on her way to Santa Ray. As he speaks to the police, Kim runs into the back room and locks the door. She attempts to open the back door, which is bolted, but the police outside manage to open it and Kim squeezes out before Garcia can get to her.

12:38A.M. Auda informs Jack that he is bringing Kate into the warehouse in a sweep pattern to avoid any further pursuit. Jack and Wallace talk. Is it true what Wallace has heard? That Jack is a born killer?

12:44 A.M. Carrie manages to get Michelle away from her desk long enough to place the filters on her system.

12:46 A.M. Novick informs the President of Jack Bauer's recent actions. Can they really trust the instincts of this agent – it appears he's had a nervous breakdown. Novick stresses that they have incontrovertible evidence and they must act on it. Palmer is still not convinced and urges his Chief of Staff to find Bauer.

Wallace tells Jack that he'll get the evidence as soon as Wallace is safely on the plane. Jack asks what assurances there are, and Wallace replies there are none, but he really doesn't want Jack Bauer to be tracking him down in the future. Auda arrives with Kate and Wallace tells her they're going on a journey. Kate looks to Jack and he tells her there's no choice, but promises she will not get hurt.

12:53 A.M. Michelle receives a call from somebody called Danny. He asks if everything is OK and demands to know about the bomb. Michelle replies that she can't tell him anything, and he gets angry, asking if she even cares about the kids. He tells her that maybe he'll ask Carrie what's going on. Listening in on the conversation, Carrie has it deleted from the logs.

The police storm the convenience store and shoot Garcia. Kim is horrified.

12:56 A.M. Lynne and Novick speak with the Vice President, who is demanding to know what is going on. Novick tells him the President wants the option of pulling out if the evidence proves to be false. The Vice President asks if Novick feels the President can do the hard thing when it comes to it. Novick believes he can. After the call, Novick tells Lynne that if Palmer calls off the operation based on Jack Bauer's speculation, it will be a disaster.

12:58 A.M. Wallace forces Kate into the boot of the car. As he prepares to leave, Auda tells Jack that the tracker is in place. As Wallace gets into the car, the three of them come under fire. Tick tick tick...

CTU INCIDENT REPORT

Haven't I Seen You Somewhere Before?: Alan Dale (Vice President Prescott) is, literally, a legend in his own lunchtime. He will be familiar to students and housewives alike for playing Jim Robinson in *Neighbours* for years. Dale became a grand master of the line 'Why Lucy, you've grown,' when his daughter was recast three times. For those surprised at Dale's graduation to grown up telly, since *Neighbours* he has found much success in America with recurring roles in *ER* and *The X-Files* as well as donning Romulan make-up alongside Jude Ciccolella as Praetor Hiren in *Star Trek: Nemesis* (2002). Sterling Macer Jr (Deputy Raynes) played Jerome Sprout in *Dragon: The Bruce Lee Story* (1993).

Time Checks: Jack tells Kate he was called **ten minutes** ago by the unknown man. At approximately **12:06 A.M.**, the Vice President indicates that the planes will be dropping their payloads in a little over **four hours**.

Fashion Police: The Vice President has a very nice suit. The tailoring budget on *24* must be much higher than that of *Neighbours*. The best way to embarrass Alan Dale would probably be to show him the title sequence of *The Young Doctors* circa 1979 where the actor sported a really nasty Afro style. Nice to see the move to the US has brought better haircuts.

The Perils Of Kim: The moral of this week's tale in the continuing adventures of Kim is: 'The world is full of assholes.' Between Gary Matheson (wonder what happened to him?), Miguel, Lonnie and Garcia, Kim has been surrounded by dorks for most of the day, with Garcia being the worst of the crop. Why Kim doesn't just pistol whip this pussy's ass right back to Burbank is a mystery. You're a Bauer, girl, opening a can of whupass comes naturally.

Alternatively, in the case of Garcia, this week's motto could also be: 'Sometimes you just have to give somebody a slap.'

It's Not Easy Being Jack: 'I don't know what else to do, I'm running out of time.' If ever there was a line that summed up *24*, that is it, perfectly encompassing the life of Jack Bauer. By giving Kate up to Wallace, Jack has, of course, turned down a definite snog. There's no way she'll go anywhere with the scumbag after this – until he comes and saves her with seconds to spare, of course. It's nice to see Jack finally getting a new buddy to play cops and robbers with in the form of Yusuf Auda. They actually make quite a fetching pair in their natty jackets, running around with cool mobile phones that double as walkie-talkies. Isn't being a secret agent just so… neat?

Great Lines:

Wallace (to Jack): 'I was down at Bening when Samuels tried to recruit you. He was real disappointed you turned him down. Said you were a born killer. Is that true?'

Death Count: One unfortunate convenience store owner brings our tally up to 79.

DEBRIEF

This is an improvement on last week's outing, but it still feels like the writing staff have put the plane on autopilot to have a quick coffee before getting down to the business of pushing the show on to the final lap. We're not quite there yet, and there are more questions that need answers before we're done. The introduction of the Vice President adds a new dimension to Palmer, and is somebody else that we don't trust an inch, although there's definitely something dodgy going on with Novick. Obviously, when

Lynne Kresge shoots everyone down with a machine gun in the final episode, these words will be eaten along with many others. And, whilst we're about it, what the hell is going on with Michelle? Is she in fact married, which seems to be the case, and is happy to be a cheating little minx with Tony? Blimey.

Pulse-Rate: 103 bpm

Questions Arising:

? Why is Novick so keen to discredit Bauer?
? Where do the Vice President's loyalties lie?
? Who is Danny, and what connects him to Michelle and Carrie?
? Who is the gunman on the roof working for?

Production Code: 2AFF18
Written by Joel Surnow and Michael Loceff
Directed by Jon Cassar

> *'The following takes place between 1:00A.M. and 2:00A.M.... Events occur in real time.'*

Guest Starring: Reiko Aylesworth (Michelle Dessler), Lourdes Benedicto (Carrie Turner), Jude Ciccolella (Mike Novick), Michelle Forbes (Lynne Kresge), Donnie Keshawarz (Yusuf Auda), Sterling Macer Jr (Deputy Raynes), Gregg Henry (Jonathan Wallace), Innis Casey (Miguel), Peter Gregory (Dr Spire), Victor Rivers (Sgt Amis), Michael Jannetta (Angry Man), Claudia DiFolco (Female Reporter), Rick Lozano (Male Reporter), Misty Carlisle (Nurse Clara)

FIELD REPORT

01:00A.M. Gunfire continues to rain down on Jack, Kate and Wallace, forcing them back inside the warehouse. Yusuf takes cover outside. Wallace believes their attackers are a team sent by his employers to kill him. Yusuf returns to the SUV to reload and rearm (with a very big gun). He checks in with Jack and advises him of the situation outside. Jack wants to call Michelle to get satellite information on the area, but Wallace orders him not to. Yusuf advises that another vehicle has arrived with more men – they are surrounded and running out of time. Wallace finally capitulates and Jack calls Michelle. She agrees to provide infrared satellite on their surrounding area, but it might take some time as she is being monitored.

01:05A.M. As Garcia is driven off in an ambulance, Kim tells the deputy that the gun was hers and that the shooting was an accident. She tells him that she escaped from police custody earlier that evening and she's a suspect for murder.

District Headquarters, Los Angeles Palmer watches a news broadcast covering the growing civil unrest as a result of the bomb's detonation. Palmer enquires as to the alert status of the National Guard – they are ready to be deployed in all major cities, but it's possible that the military may have to be called in to assist. Palmer asks for the army to be put on alert, and he'll deal with the consequences later. Lynne briefs him on the position of the bombers. Michelle continues to work on the satellite information. Carrie asks her what she's doing, and Michelle evades her question, asking her to finish prepping files for the next shift. Suspicious, Carrie goes to see if Tony needs any help.

01:08A.M. Carrie tells Tony that Michelle was searching through satellite data just after she received a call that wouldn't lock on to their trace. Tony wonders if it could be legitimate, but asks Carrie to find out what Michelle is up to. Yusuf advises Jack that their attackers appear to be repositioning themselves. They are still awaiting the satellite data from Michelle and Jack tells him to hang tight. Kate asks Jack why Wallace needs her. Jack explains that with her father's connections to the CIA, the company has a special travel dispensation and Wallace needs Kate to get out of the country. Kate tells him that she'd need to be on-board the plane at take-off, and Jack assures her that will not happen. At CTU, Carrie observes Michelle sorting through satellite data.

01:15A.M. Kim is transferred back to LA in a squad car. She asks if she can find out how her boyfriend is. The officer tells her that she is under arrest and that she'd better keep quiet. She'll be able to make a phone call at the station. She asks what the point is, as she has nobody to call. Carrie calls Tony, informing him that Michelle is still going through the infrared satellite data. He asks her for the co-ordinates as that's where they'll find Jack. Carrie can't do that as Michelle has been looking at multiple quadrants to cover her tracks. Tony says he'll take care of it.

01:16A.M. Michelle disappears into the bathroom to call Jack. She downloads the satellite data straight into his PDA, and tells him that he might not be able to stay anonymous for much longer as Tony is getting suspicious. She leaves the bathroom and walks straight into Tony, who is waiting for her. He asks where Jack is, and she tells him she doesn't know. She also tells him to call President Palmer to advise him not to act on the Cyprus recordings until Jack has finished his investigation. Tony asks her once again, forcefully this time, where Jack is. Once again, Michelle maintains that she doesn't know, and walks away.

Jack and Wallace plan their route from the building to the car. It will be risky. Jack gives Kate a gun and tells her to stay behind him, before calling Yusuf to brief him on the position of the shooters.

01:20A.M. Lynne has spoken with the Secretary of Defence, who wants to know how long they are going to give Jack Bauer to disprove the Cyprus recording. Palmer insists that he will give Bauer up until the time the planes start releasing their bombs and that there will be no pre-strike in the meantime. Novick asks the President to join him as there is a situation that needs his attention. Civil unrest that appears to be motivated against citizens of Middle Eastern origins is springing up along the East Coast. A new report is piped in from Atlanta, where a member of the local militia announces that he considers they are in a war situation and will do what it takes to protect America from naturalised Middle Eastern citizens. Novick informs Palmer that the National Guard doesn't have enough manpower to keep the situation in check. Palmer orders the entire Georgia National Guard to the flashpoint in Atlanta – that's where they'll show the media how they respond to racism and xenophobia within their own country.

01:27 A.M. On Jack's signal, Yusuf puts down a carpet of smoke bombs in the alleyway. Jack, Kate and Wallace leave the warehouse as Yusuf begins to lay down covering fire. They fight their way through the gauntlet of the alleyway under heavy fire. Yusuf pulls up in the SUV, and as they climb in and drive away, Wallace is hit. There is no exit wound, but Wallace refuses to be taken to a hospital and orders Jack to drive to LAX.

Palmer watches further news footage of the civil disturbance. The National Guard are on containment orders only, but Palmer wants their action stepped up and law to be enforced. Novick believes that declaring a curfew would help to get everybody off the streets, and Palmer agrees. He will address the public in a few minutes.

01:32 A.M. Tony advises Carrie that the police have responded to an incident of gunfire in Studio City. He confronts Michelle – is that Jack's location? He wants to speak to Bauer now. Michelle advises against it, as it could jeopardise Jack's current situation. Tony has had enough of playing games, and Michelle finally puts him through to Jack. Jack tells Tony to keep out of things, but advises him of their current status. Tony feels that Wallace may be using them, but Jack thinks that the attack proves his story. Tony tells him to bring Wallace to CTU, but Jack hangs up.

01:38A.M. Kim is led into the police station, where the desk officer takes charge of her. He goes through Kim's file, telling her that she's off the hook. They know that Gary Matheson killed Carla and they are currently searching for him, and they now know she was telling the truth about the bomb. The officer recommends that somebody from CTU should call the DA on her behalf, but she's free to go.

01:40A.M. As they speed towards the airport, Kate calls the charter company to arrange the flight. Wallace, still bleeding badly, tells her he wants to go to Indonesia. The flight arranged, Wallace falls unconscious. Jack pulls up the location of a medical care centre on the SUV's computer, and orders Yusuf to drive straight there.

01:42A.M. Tony receives a call from Kim. She tells him she might need some help from CTU in speaking to the DA, but that she's OK. Tony tells her he knows that she'd rather be speaking to her father, but he's still out in the field, forgetting that Kim doesn't know he didn't go down with the plane.

01:43A.M. Jack and his team pull up at the urgent care centre and drag Wallace inside. Jack is forced to pull his gun on a doctor in order to gain entry. Wallace is placed on a gurney, and Jack tells the doctor that he must keep him alive as he has vital information of national security. Kim calls Miguel at the hospital. He isn't exactly pleased to hear from her, and he tells her that it's over. Kim wants to go to see him, but he refuses and hangs up, leaving Kim confused. As Miguel lies in bed, it is revealed that he has lost a leg.

01:51A.M. Michelle speaks to Tony to apologise. Tony isn't really in the mood to hear what she has to say. CTU is supposed to be supporting the President, and if he can't account for his agents, then all they have is chaos. They don't have Jack, they don't have proof, they don't have anything. Michelle apologises again and leaves.

01:53A.M. Palmer is briefed on the current position of the bombers, and is assured that the planes can be ordered back at any time. Palmer is shocked when Novick informs him that a young boy has been killed by the National Guard in their response to the situation in Atlanta.

01:55 A.M. Jack and the doctor examine the X-rays taken of Wallace. The doctor tells Jack that he will be unable to remove the bullet without surgery. They don't have time for that and Jack asks the doctor to do what he can now. Yusuf, ever the optimist, believes that Wallace is going to die. Jack replies that they'd better hope he doesn't. The doctor numbs the area around the wound and begins to work. Wallace pushes the doctor away. He pulls Jack close and tells him that he won't make it. As Wallace begins to die, Jack desperately asks him where the evidence is. Wallace manages to breath that it's on a memory chip, but dies before he can say where. Defeated, Jack turns away. As he looks on, he notices something on Wallace's X-ray, and asks for a scalpel. He cuts away at the dead soldier's body and pulls out a memory chip hidden under the skin. They have their evidence. Tick, tick, tick…

CTU INCIDENT REPORT

Haven't I Seen You Somewhere Before?: Peter Gregory (Dr Spire) has appeared in the film *Mouse Hunt* (1997) and made guest appearances in *Chicago Hope*, *Murder, She Wrote*, and *ER*. You can probably see his arse in *Red Shoe Diaries 12: Girl on a Bike* (2000). Victor Rivers has provided voices for *Batman Beyond*, played Joaquin Murrieta in *The Mask Of Zorro* (1998) and appeared alongside Kiefer Sutherland in *Twin Peaks: Fire Walk With Me* (1992).

Time Checks: At approximately **01:07 A.M.**, Lynne informs Palmer that the bombers will enter Middle Eastern airspace in **four or five hours** (in other words, about ten minutes into episode 23 (**6 A.M. – 7 A.M.**). On leaving the warehouse, Jack, Kate and Wallace will have **ten seconds** to get to the car. At **01:53 A.M.** Palmer is advised that the first planes will be reaching their targets in just under three hours. OK, let's see – that means they'll start dropping bombs just in time for the cliffhanger to **4:00 A.M. – 5:00 A.M.** The charter plane arranged by Kate is set to depart at **03:45 A.M.**

Fashion Police: With no major new characters being introduced this week, there's an absence of fashion felonies. It's all cop uniforms and white coats. Is this category in danger of becoming obsolete?

The Perils Of Kim: The Lord giveth, and the Lord taketh away! In the space of five minutes, Kim regains a father from the dead, then gets dumped like a lame dog in the street by her kick-boxing boyfriend. Um, it doesn't look like Miguel will be doing much kickboxing anytime soon, what with half a leg missing and all. Miguel, we understand your pain, we really do, but you're being a tad unfair to Kim. You didn't have to go along with her crazy stories about bombs blowing up, did you? And let's not dodge the issue here. What kind of moron thinks it's a good idea to set fire to a bandanna in the back of a car in the hope that the cop might stop to put it out? Oh, that was you, wasn't it? So really, mate, your current impersonation of Long John Silver is down to you. Another word of advice: Kim is really hot.

It's Not Easy Being Jack: Don't you just love it when Jack pulls his gun on the cute nurse at the door of the medical centre? If he didn't have his arms full of a bloodied nearly corpse, we'd all want to shake his hand for that one. Aside from that, there's not a lot else for Jack to do this week apart from piss off Tony some more, and rip memory chips out of dead marines. Did anyone else think he was going to start crying like a four-year-old when Wallace died?

Great Lines:
Palmer: 'If this is where it's gonna start, this is where it's gonna stop!'
Nurse: 'Sir, I will call the police!'
Jack (pulling his gun): 'Lady, I am the police!'

Death Count: This is a difficult one – so many bodies go down in a hail of gunfire this week that it's hard to keep track. Tony says that the police have found four bodies at the warehouse, but this doesn't tally with what happens on screen – in the shooting that takes place at the episode's opening, five attackers appear to go down. Then the body count really ratchets up as Jack and co escape from the warehouse, taking out seven bad guys in their dash for the car. Add the unfortunate Jonathan Wallace to this count, and that gives an episode total of 13, making a series total so far of 92. For those of you who want to nitpick on this point, we're not counting the two off-screen deaths caused by the National Guard in their response to the civil unrest.

Trivia: Fans who are looking to deck out their home in essential CTU chic may like to know that the lamp in Tony Almeida's office is available from Ikea.

DEBRIEF

As an episode, this sits somewhere between pushing the plot forward nicely and having our characters sitting around offices, conference rooms and police stations doing not very much at all. The most satisfying plot strand revolves around Jack and his merry band of adventurers, and this is full of jolly action pieces in which the lads get to fire their guns a lot. Yusuf has the most fun, tooling up with lots of hardware and getting to chuck smoke bombs around with gay abandon. Kate finally stops being the dumb blonde damsel in distress and shows she has some balls by taking out a bad guy.

What also impresses is how the writers are not shying away from showing the social impact of a dirty great bomb being detonated, and the civil unrest that begins to sweep the East Coast has a definite sense of realism behind it. Palmer's reaction to the death of the young boy is beautifully played by Dennis Haysbert.

And what of Kim? Elisha Cuthbert continues to play well with badly pitched curve balls, which is all credit to a talented actress. Surely her storyline has been exhausted and it's about time she was brought back to the relative safety of CTU for a cup of coffee and a doughnut? And please, will somebody slap Tony. He's being very mean to Michelle and in all probability just turned down a definite snog when he chucks her out of his office.

Unusually for an episode of *24*, this hour finishes with something of a resolution rather than a cliffhanger. Jack has retrieved the prize he's been playing for for the last few episodes, and with six episodes to go, it feels like we've just hit the home straight.

Pulse-Rate: 110 bpm

Questions Arising:

- Why is everyone so keen to have Palmer continue with the mission?
- Will Michelle and Tony ever get it together?
- Will the memory chip contain what Jack needs?

Production Code: 2AFF19
Written by Howard Gordon
Directed by James Whitmore Jr

> ***'The following takes place between 2:00A.M. and 3:00A.M.... Events occur in real time.'***

Guest Starring: Reiko Aylesworth (Michelle Dessler), Tobin Bell (Peter Kingsley), Jude Ciccolella (Mike Novick), Michelle Forbes (Lynne Kresge), Lourdes Benedicto (Carrie Turner), Donnie Keshawarz (Yusuf Auda), Gregg Henry (Jonathan Wallace), Alan Dale (Vice President Prescott), Nick Offerman (Marcus), Justin Louis (Danny Dessler), Paul Schulze (Ryan Chappelle), Carmen Argenziano (General Gratz), Raymond Cruz (Rouse), Mark Ivanir (Stark)

FIELD REPORT

02:00A.M. Palmer is briefed, along with the Joint Chiefs and Vice President, on the current status of the planned mission. The Vice President questions whether Palmer is still behind the action as he's sensing some caution. Palmer outlines that Jack Bauer is currently searching for evidence that may disprove the Cyprus recording, but the Vice President points out that Bauer has yet to produce this evidence. If the first strike is delayed, it could add 20,000 U.S. casualties to the list. With those numbers presented to him, Palmer sees no choice but to proceed as planned.

As Yusuf examines the memory chip, Jack attempts to get through to the President, but is told Palmer is unavailable. He then calls Tony at CTU.

02:03A.M. Tony orders Jack to bring Wallace back to CTU. Jack tells him that Wallace is dead, but he has the evidence, which he'll bring to CTU. Jack urges Toby to call the President to let him know what's going on. Yusuf finds a tracker embedded in the memory chip, meaning that whoever wanted to stop Wallace from leaving the country can find their location. He believes he can remove the tracker without destroying the audio file.

02:05A.M. Michelle takes another call from Danny. He asks her what's going on, but, as before, she can't tell him. Danny hangs up. Tony informs her that Jack has the memory chip and is on his way in. Michelle asks if the President knows, but Tony refuses to call him until they have verified the evidence.

As Yusuf works on the chip, a vehicle pulls up outside the medical centre – somebody has just come looking for the chip. If Yusuf removes the tracker, Jack thinks he can use it to lure the men away, allowing Yusuf and Kate to get to CTU with the evidence. As the men make their way inside the building, Yusuf removes the tracker and Jack advises a meeting point. He tells Yusuf if he doesn't make it, they should head to CTU without him. Jack heads off with the tracker. The men make their way through the building, picking up Jack's signal. One of them notices Wallace's dead body lying on the gurney and enters the room to investigate. Yusuf and Kate hide in the connecting room. The man discovers that the chip has been removed from Wallace's corpse, and leaves to catch up with his colleagues. Yusuf and Kate come out of hiding and leave the medical centre.

02:13 A.M. As Novick briefs the President on further incidents of civil unrest, Lynne interrupts with a call from Tony. Over speakerphone, Tony advises of the possibility that they may have the evidence to disprove the Cyprus recordings. Novick wonders about Tony's new-found confidence in Jack, but Tony believes that Jack had no choice in taking the course of action he did. They should have the evidence within the hour, which they will then verify. After speaking with Tony, Palmer suddenly announces his intention to call off the attack. Novick and Lynne urge him to reconsider, but Palmer asks them, what if Jack Bauer is right? Novick counters – what if Jack Bauer is wrong? Stopping and restarting the mission could cost thousands of lives. Palmer has made his decision. He asks for a conference with the Joint Chiefs. Tony lets Michelle know that he called the President to let him know about the memory chip. Michelle tells him that he did the right thing.

02:18 A.M. Yusuf and Kate drive to CTU. Kate is unable to get through to CTU – the phone system is overloaded. Yusuf wonders if the problem is at CTU's end. Perhaps they are gearing up for the war against his country. Kate tells him there won't be a war, but he wonders if she'd think differently if her family were being threatened. The three men trace the tracker to the basement of the medical centre, where they find it discarded, minus the memory chip. Through the basement window, they spot Jack making a run for it, and a back-up team is called in to intercept. Cars converge on Jack's position, and he manages to take one of the men out, but is then floored by a taser. Jack is dragged back inside the medical centre.

02:25 A.M. Lynne arrives at Novick's office to find the Chief of

Staff fielding an angry call about the President's decision to call off the attack. She asks him if he knows anything about a cabinet meeting called by the Vice President. Novick wonders if it could involve the President's recent actions and asks if she's told the President about this. She hasn't, as she was waiting to find out more. Novick tells her he'll ask around.

02:26 A.M. Jack is being tortured in the basement of the medical centre. He has been forced to vomit so his stomach contents can be scanned for the chip. One of the men receives a phone call from an unnamed man flying in a chopper. He asks to speak to Jack. Jack is hoisted to his feet by chains and the phone pushed to his ear. The man makes Jack an offer – the chip for a very large sum of money. Jack tells him it's not for sale and his answer is final. The phone is passed to Stark, the man who is carrying out the torture. He says he'll get an answer from Jack, but the man in the chopper is not as confident – he knows how tough Jack Bauer is.

02:29 A.M. Stark takes a scalpel from his collection and waves it in front of Jack's face. He asks once again where the chip is, but Jack remains quiet. Stark sets to work with the scalpel.

02:30 A.M. Michelle asks Carrie to help her in accessing the CBP software so she can start verifying the chip as soon as Jack arrives. Carrie tells her to send it through to her screen and she'll take care of it, but Michelle just wants her to access the software. As an argument breaks out between them, Tony calls down and asks Michelle to join him upstairs. He asks Michelle exactly what bad blood there is between her and Carrie. Michelle reluctantly tells him that when she worked at Division, she and Carrie were friends. She introduced Carrie to her brother, who left his wife and kids for her. Carrie soon grew bored and dumped him, leaving him with no job or family, causing him to attempt suicide. Tony sympathises, but tells her that the pair have to find a way of working together. A call comes through to Tony's office – it's for Michelle. Her brother is in reception.

02:33A.M. Danny Dessler is led into CTU. He wanted to see his sister and apologise for his earlier behaviour. Michelle tells him he has to leave, but he spots Carrie talking to Tony. He starts shouting at her, and walks towards her. Michelle tries to calm him down, but he dives forward and attempts to strangle Carrie. Tony and the security guards pull him off and Danny is dragged away.

02:38A.M. Novick takes Lynne to one side. The meeting is taking place – the Vice President has been calling cabinet members personally. He has a meeting set up with a source within the Defence Department in a room nearby, and against Novick's wishes, Lynne insists on being present. Medics attend to Carrie, and Tony notices Michelle disappearing down a corridor. He catches up with her and finds her crying. He assures her that everything will be OK. They end up kissing, and Carrie interrupts them. Chappelle is looking for Tony.

Jack's torture continues – very painfully. Stark holds up a plastic bottle for Jack to see, melting it through with a soldering iron. Guess what's coming next! As the soldering iron sears into Jack's flesh, he blacks out. One of the men stops Stark from continuing. Stark tells the man never to touch him again, and is about to continue when the phone rings. It is the man from the chopper. He asks if they've made any progress, and is disappointed with the answer. He reminds Stark that there is a time issue, and that he needs the chip.

02:46A.M. Novick meets Lynne. He confirms that the Vice President has indeed set up a cabinet meeting. He outlines Section Four of the Twenty-Fifth Amendment, which states that if the majority feel the President is unfit to carry out his duties, then he can be removed and the Vice President will take his place. He asks Lynne where she stands on the President's decision to halt the attack, and she is distraught that he would question her loyalty. Novick pushes her on this – she must be absolutely sure. She is. Novick calls in a man called Eisberg and leaves, telling Lynne he is sorry. Lynne suddenly realises that Novick is part of the conspiracy and Eisberg stops her from leaving. He throws her back into the room and locks the door. Novick tells him not to let her out and walks away. Lynne's shouted protests follow him down the corridor.

02:53 A.M. Kate listens to radio news reports of escalating racial violence as she and Yusuf wait for Jack. Yusuf thinks it's time they headed for CTU as they've waited longer than they should have. As he reverses back, he is forced to stop as a fire engine speeds past. He asks Kate if she's OK, but is suddenly pulled out of the vehicle by two men. They call him a 'towel head' and accuse his people of trying to kill them with the bomb. They start to beat him, but Yusuf pulls his gun and orders the men to lie on the ground, telling Kate to get back in the SUV. Another man comes up behind Yusuf and smashes his head with a brick. Kate tries to help, but is thrown aside, and the men continue to beat Yusuf.

Tony calls Ryan Chappelle. He is unhappy when Chappelle tells him he is en route to CTU with some key personnel from Division.

02:56 A.M. After speaking to Chappelle, Tony calls Michelle to see if her brother is OK. Michelle apologises for their earlier game of tonsil tennis, but Tony says he's glad it happened. Michelle is worried that Carrie will make trouble for them, but Tony says he'll deal with her. Jack screams in agony as the torture continues, losing consciousness. One of the men thinks they should give Jack a minute to recover, but Stark orders him to wake Jack up. Holding up a taser, Stark asks Jack about his daughter. Does he want Kim to be an orphan? Jack doesn't reply, and Stark gives the taser to the other man, who uses it on Jack. The man refuses to do it a second time, and Stark takes the taser and uses it himself. Jack loses consciousness, and Stark wants him woken again. Jack doesn't come round. He's dead. Tick, tick, tick...

CTU INCIDENT REPORT

Haven't I Seen You Somewhere Before?: Tobin Bell (Peter Kingsley) has guest starred in numerous TV series, from *The Equaliser* through to *The West Wing*. His film appearances include *Mississippi Burning* (1988), *Goodfellas* (1990) and the voice of Zaragoza in *The Road To El Dorado* (2000). Nick Offerman (Marcus) is engaged to *Will and Grace* star Megan Mullalley. He has guest starred in *Will and Grace*, *ER* and *The West Wing*. Justin Louis (Danny Dessler) has guest starred in many genre TV shows, including *Millennium*, *Star Trek: Voyager* and *The Outer Limits*. Paul Schulze (Ryan Chappelle) is perhaps best known for his recurring role as Father Phillip Intintola in *The Sopranos* and plays Officer Rick Heim in the popular prison drama, *Oz*. Sci-fi fans will know Carmen Argenziano from his recurring role as Sam Carter's father in *Stargate SG-1*, and will doubtless recognise him from many TV and film roles in a career that stretches back over 30 years.

Time Checks: The medical centre is **40 minutes** away from CTU. Jack tells Yusuf if he's not at the meeting point in **15 minutes**, he and Kate are to leave without him. The Vice President calls a cabinet meeting **an hour and half** from approximately **02:25 A.M.** Chappelle advises Tony that he'll be arriving at CTU in **30 minutes**.

Fashion Police: Kingsley (that's the chap in the helicopter whose name we haven't learnt yet) is obviously a bad guy. He has a nicely cut suit, gets ferried around in a personal chopper and has a swish penthouse apartment, just like every villain should. His henchmen out in the field, on the other hand, should be ashamed. Call themselves terrorists? There isn't even one decent goatee beard amongst them, and Stark, the supposedly evil torturer, looks like he just stepped out of a library.

The Perils Of Kim: It would take a feat of unbelievable stupidity for Kim to find herself in danger this week, mainly down to the fact that she isn't in the episode. Of course, next week we'll probably find her trapped in a burning building, surrounded by rabid dogs and on the run from international terrorists who want her to autograph that issue of *FHM*. The moral of this week's tale is: 'Sometimes we all just need a week off.'

It's Not Easy Being Jack: It really isn't easy being Jack this week, is it? The poor guy has been put through the blender in the past, but nothing like this. He's electrocuted, beaten, sliced, burnt, forced to throw his guts up and finally he dies. Surely this day can't get any worse? Wanna bet?

Great Lines:

Palmer: 'So what are you saying, Mike? That I should continue with a military operation just to prove I'm decisive?'

Jack: 'It's not for sale.'
Kingsley: 'If someone wants to buy it, it's for sale.'

Death Count: Jack takes out one of the bad guys before attempting his *Starsky and Hutch* slide over a car bonnet, but then Jack gets killed in return. Counting Jack, the death count stands at 94.

DEBRIEF

Does this episode of *24* contain the ultimate cliffhanger? The death of Jack Bauer is an audacious climax, but somehow it seems likely he'll be back in the land of the living next week. It's very convenient for Jack that the bad guys chose to torture him in a fully equipped medical centre.

The players are lining up for the final stretch. Ryan Chappelle is on his way to CTU, Novick reveals his true colours (no surprise there then), and we're getting closer to the real villains with the appearance of the mysterious man in the helicopter. As always there are more questions to answer, which keeps that 24-hour clock ticking along nicely.

A refreshing note to the episode is that after 18 weeks of sheer hell, Kim gets some time out, which, in terms of story credibility, was a necessary and welcome move. If she's on her way back to CTU, which seems likely, it's possible Kim may play a greater role in the central storyline. And finally, a big up for Tony and Michelle finally having the snog that's been brewing since episode one. Hurrah!

Pulse-Rate: 115 bpm

Questions Arising:

? Who is the man in the chopper?

? Will Vice President Prescott succeed in ousting Palmer?

? What the hell is Mike Novick up to?

Production Code: 2AFF20
Written by Neil Cohen
Directed by James Whitmore Jr

'The following takes place between 3:00A.M. and 4:00A.M.... Events occur in real time.'

Guest Starring: Reiko Aylesworth (Michelle Dessler), Tobin Bell (Peter Kingsley), Jude Ciccolella (Mike Novick), Lourdes Benedicto (Carrie Turner), Michelle Forbes (Lynne Kresge), Donnie Keshawarz (Yusuf Auda), Alan Dale (Vice President Prescott), Nick Offerman (Marcus), Raymond Cruz (Rouse), Paul Schulze (Ryan Chappelle), Glenn Morshower (Agent Aaron Pierce), Mark Ivanir (Stark)

FIELD REPORT

03:00A.M. As Stark frantically works to revive Jack, his henchman searches for epinephrine upstairs. He is interrupted by a doctor and patient. The doctor asks what he's doing, and the man calmly kills the patient and drags the doctor downstairs to help. Kingsley phones to speak to Stark, but O'Hara takes the call. He has no choice but to tell him that Jack is flatlining. Kingsley hopes that Stark can fix whatever he broke, but if he can't, O'Hara should do it himself. The doctor is dragged in and at gunpoint he administers the epinephrine directly to Jack's heart, before attempting to shock him. Jack fails to respond, but after the third attempt, they get a heartbeat. O'Hara shoots Stark before turning to the now conscious Jack to ask where the chip is.

03:05A.M. Novick speaks to Vice President Prescott via satellite phone. He tells him that Lynne Kresge is currently under guard and that Palmer is still in the dark. Novick expresses some doubt about their actions, but Prescott assures him that history will recognise they did the right thing. Palmer walks into the office. The President knows his Chief of Staff doesn't agree with his decision to halt the attack, but thanks him for his loyalty. Palmer needs to brief Lynne, and Novick tells him he'll see if he can find her. Lynne continues to bang on the door of her prison, but to no avail. She manages to open a locker in the room, and finds a working blowtorch among some tools.

03:08A.M. The men who attacked Yusuf and Kate go through Yusuf's pockets. They take some money and the memory chip. Kate staggers to her feet and demands the chip back. She has money, and her house isn't far away. The men agree, and bundle Kate into the car. Badly hurt, Yusuf drags himself painfully to a nearby phone box and tries to make a call. All the lines are busy. O'Hara orders the doctor to inject Jack with Beroglide, a drug that will paralyse his diaphragm. Kingsley calls again, and as O'Hara is distracted, Jack begs the doctor to help him escape. The doctor, fearing for his life, reluctantly agrees and begins to loosen Jack's bonds. O'Hara returns and orders the doctor to inject the Beroglide, which he does. Jack begins to gag in pain.

03:18 A.M. Ryan Chappelle arrives at CTU and Michelle informs him that most of the phones are down and they are relying on SATCOM. Chappelle commends Tony for not letting Jack change their position on the Cyprus recordings. Tony believes that they have to eliminate any reasonable doubt, but Chappelle doesn't want to hear it. He lets Tony know that his promotion to director of CTU doesn't have to be permanent. Using the blowtorch, Lynne ignites a waste bin of paper. The flames set off the smoke alarm, and Eisberg unlocks the door to investigate, to find Lynne and a heavy fire extinguisher in the face waiting for him. Lynne runs down the corridor, the stunned Eisberg not far behind. He catches up with her on the stairwell, and after a struggle, Lynne is thrown over the banister, falling several floors. She lies unconscious on the floor.

03:21 A.M. Palmer is having difficulty getting through to Prescott, who appears to be unavailable. Concerned, Palmer seeks the counsel of Secret Service Agent Aaron Pierce. As an agent with 20 years experience, he asks if Pierce knows of a plot against him. Is Prescott after his Presidency? Pierce tells Palmer that he has good instincts and should listen to them.

03:23 A.M. Kingsley receives a visit from two men, who tell him that Max isn't happy. Kingsley tells them not to worry. The President will change his decision over the attack, and Bauer won't be a problem. The men leave.

03:24 A.M. When Jack refuses to talk, O'Hara orders the doctor to double the dose of Beroglide. As the doctor prepares the syringe, Jack begins to talk, quietly, bringing O'Hara closer so he can hear. As Jack talks, the doctor slams the syringe into O'Hara's back. The terrorist starts to gag and falls to his knees. Jack staggers up from the gurney and takes his gun, firing it once to bring O'Hara's two henchmen into the room. Jack calmly shoots them down. O'Hara has 15 minutes of choking death ahead if him, and Jack promises to make it quick if he tells him who was on the other end of the phone. O'Hara croaks: 'Peter Kingsley' before Jack shoots him.

03:32 A.M. Palmer voices his concerns to Novick over not being able to reach Prescott in Washington. Novick promises to get him on the phone as soon as possible. Palmer asks that Lynne go over his statement, and Novick assures him that he'll pass the draft copy on to her. He leaves Palmer and rushes to his own office.

03:33 A.M. Novick immediately calls Prescott over SATCOM. He informs the Vice President that Palmer is getting suspicious, and that he should start returning Palmer's calls. Prescott urges Novick to keep Palmer off his back for a little while longer; they're nearly there.

03:35 A.M. Jack walks barefoot through the medical centre. He calls Michelle at CTU to let her know that Yusuf and Kate have the chip and he is proceeding to their agreed rendezvous point. The connection is bad and the call is disconnected. Michelle informs Tony that she thinks Jack tried to call, and they will attempt to trace the number. Chappelle warns Tony against assigning resources to the Bauer situation, but Tony feels they should give Jack some leeway – he may have evidence that proves the Cyprus recordings are faked. Chappelle wonders when this evidence is going to be produced.

Palmer and Novick speak to Vice President Prescott. Palmer gives Prescott the opportunity to be open about his opinions on the attack being aborted, knowing that his Vice President was vocally opposed to the decision. Prescott maintains his protests were levelled behind closed doors and he has betrayed no confidences. Palmer gives him the chance to tell him about anything else, but Prescott reveals nothing. As the call ends, Palmer opines to Novick that he still doesn't trust Prescott. The men are interrupted by Agent Pierce, who informs them that Lynne Kresge has been critically injured.

03:42 A.M. Michelle has traced Jack's call to somewhere between Encino and Studio City. Tony asks Michelle to monitor police channels to see if they can work out where he was heading. Carrie has overheard their conversation.

03:43 A.M. Jack arrives at the arranged meeting point and finds Yusuf collapsed in the phone box, battered and bloody. He mumbles that Kate has taken the men to her home in Hancock Park, where she will trade money for the chip. Jack attempts to drag Yusuf from the phone box, but he dies. Jack tells him he's sorry and leaves, driving fast for Hancock Park.

03:44 A.M. Kate and her attackers arrive at the house. When they open the door, the alarm begins to sound, but Kate gives them the code to shut it off. One of the men orders her to get the money, and Kate leads them into the house. Palmer and Novick catch up with the medical team rushing Lynne into an ambulance. She is in a critical condition and has been slipping in and out of consciousness. Palmer wants to speak to her, but Novick thinks it's a bad idea (hmm, wonder why?). Palmer asks her what happened. Lynne attempts to say the word *Novick*, but is unable to speak, and tries to point at the Chief of Staff instead. He takes her hand quickly, as if to comfort her. She is loaded on to the ambulance, Palmer none the wiser that Novick is part of the conspiracy.

03:52 A.M. Driving to find Kate, Jack is still unable to get through to CTU on his mobile phone. Carrie attempts to blackmail Tony. She knows that he and Michelle are spending their time searching for Jack, and in return for not telling Chappelle what they're up to, she demands a promotion to give her seniority over Michelle. Tony calls Chappelle over and tells him what Carrie has just asked for. Carrie tells Chappelle what her superiors have been doing, and that she was going to tell him. Chappelle tells her to go away, and confronts Tony. He thought they were past the Bauer problem, but Tony counters him – he is allocating reasonable resources to gathering all the facts, and if Chappelle doesn't like it, he can relieve Tony of command. Chappelle doesn't think that will be necessary, but only because he doesn't have anybody with which to replace him tonight.

Kate opens the safe in her bedroom, and the men are a little upset when she tries to give them Euros. They find $600 in cash and some jewellery, and Kate pleads with them to take it all as long as they leave the chip. The men threaten to kill her as she knows what they look like. Kate manages to run from the bedroom, the men in pursuit. They catch up with her, but as one of the men is about to shoot her, Jack appears from the darkness and drops him with a single shot. The remaining men flee down the hallway and lock themselves in the bathroom. Jack shouts that all he wants is the chip. He is told that if he comes in the room, they'll smash the chip.

At CTU, Tony briefs his team on the search for Jack. Novick watches by video conference as Prescott arrives at his secret cabinet meeting. Some of the cabinet are surprised that the meeting is closed to the President, but Prescott outlines the purpose of the meeting. He puts it to them that based on his reaction to the events of the day, David Palmer is no longer fit to hold the office of President of the United States. Tick tick tick...

CTU INCIDENT REPORT

Haven't I Seen You Somewhere Before?: Briefly reprising his role from the **Day One** of *24* is Glenn Morshower (Agent Aaron Pierce). He played the recurring role of Sheriff Brian Mobley throughout the first season of *CSI: Crime Scene Investigation*, and has also worked for director Ridley Scott in *Black Hawk Down* (2001). He regularly appears in *The West Wing* as the State Department Civilian Advisor.

Behind The Camera: Writer Neil Cohen worked as a scriptwriter on the short lived sci-fi series *Mann and Machine* in the early nineties, and wrote the screenplay for *The Disappearance of Garcia Lorca* (1997).

Time Checks: At **03:33 A.M.** Prescott asks Novick to keep Palmer busy for another **half an hour** or **45 minutes** maximum.

Fashion Police: Ryan Chappelle is obviously going to turn out to be a bad guy because his suit is too nice. No, really, take a look. The bad guys all wear nice, smartly cut suits. Would you trust a man like Prescott if he's wearing a suit like that? No way!

Whatever Happened To Kim Bauer?: Out of deference to Kim's absence for a second episode running, the category formerly known as **The Perils Of Kim** receives a new title. You remember Kim? Blonde, cute, has a startling talent for landing herself in trouble and going out with lame brain boyfriends. No?

It's Not Easy Being Jack: After a week of being hung from the ceiling in his pants, it's good to see Jack get back to some good old fashioned, erm… Jacking, for want of a better word. Is this the invention of a new verb to celebrate the actions of *24*'s psychotic secret agent hero? To Jack. I Jack, we Jack, they Jack. Anyway, if he was pissed off before, imagine the mood Jack's going to be in after dying for a couple of minutes. There's nothing like Jack Bauer emerging from the shadows as some dark angel of vengeance with a big gun in his hand. Although he might have spent the previous five minutes assessing the lighting in the house to see which doorway would make him look hotter for Kate's benefit, before saving the poor girl.

Great Lines:

Palmer: 'Aaron, is Prescott coming after me?'

Pierce: 'I'm not sure. But you have good instincts, sir. I'd listen to them if I were you.'

Palmer: 'I'm the Commander-in-Chief. When I call, there's only one direction.'

Death Count: A high body count this week sees Jack getting back into his stride. Poor old Yusuf – all he wanted was to be part of the gang, and he got ten bells kicked out of him for his trouble. Seven deaths in total this week, including that poor innocent patient at the medical centre. And we thought the NHS was bad... With seven bodies in the morgue, that brings the running tally past the century mark to 101. However, with Jack's miraculous recovery at the beginning of the episode, the count should be adjusted and brought back down to 100.

DEBRIEF

It's all getting exciting, isn't it? The best moment of this episode is the look of sphincter-clenching terror on Mike Novick's face when he hears about Lynne going for a dive off the stairs. This showcases another of *24*'s strengths in keeping characters firmly sketched in shades of grey. There are generally no blacks and whites – we know who is bad, who is good, but everybody acts with consistent motivation. Why has Mike Novick, somebody previously depicted as a decent person, suddenly turned against his friend and President, David Palmer? On the same note, is Vice President Prescott in the pocket of the oil people, or is he acting with what he believes are honourable intentions? It looks like we'll be kept guessing right up to the very end.

Other notable moments in this episode include the death of Yusuf Auda. As a character who was drafted into the narrative very late, he became a likeable member of the ensemble, working well with Jack and Kate. He'll be missed. It's also comforting to see the return of Secret Service Agent Aaron Pierce, last seen protecting David Palmer in **Day One.** It's kisses to the series's past like this that help to add layers to the *24* universe. And he's ginger too, so it's good to see minority groups well represented amongst the cast.

Finally, where the hell is Kim?

Pulse-Rate: 112 bpm

Questions Arising:

- ? Who is Max?
- ? Will Lynne survive to tell all?
- ? Is Prescott working for the oil representatives?

Production Code: 2AFF21
Written by Robert Cochran and Howard Gordon
Directed by Ian Toynton

'The following takes place between 4:00A.M. and 5:00A.M.... Events occur in real time.'

Guest Starring: Reiko Aylesworth (Michelle Dessler), Lourdes Benedicto (Carrie Turner), Jude Ciccolella (Mike Novick), Alan Dale (Vice President Prescott), Nick Offerman (Marcus), Maurice Compte (Cole), Paul Schulze (Ryan Chappelle), Glenn Morshower (Agent Aaron Pierce), Michael Holden (Ron Wieland), John Rubinstein (Secretary of State), Austin Tichenor (Secretary of Treasury), Paco Farias (Deputy Sheriff), Alex Daniels (Bryce), Harris Yulin (Roger Stanton – uncredited)

FIELD REPORT

04:00A.M. Jack pleads with the men in Kate's bathroom. He identifies himself as a federal agent, and tells them he needs the chip. In return, he'll let them go. The two men begin to argue – the chip is the only thing keeping them alive. The men start to grapple, and Jack kicks the door in, firing a warning shot. The two men surrender, and Jack picks up the chip from the floor where it fell. Kate gets some wire so they can tie up the men.

Palmer asks Novick why the bombers have yet to return to base since he gave the order to halt the attack. Novick advises that the planes are in a holding pattern, and asks the President to accompany him. Palmer isn't in the habit of going anywhere, and Novick explains that certain members of the cabinet are questioning whether he is fit to continue as Chief Executive of the U.S. Palmer is visibly taken aback, but remains calm, accompanying his Chief of Staff to the conference room.

04:04A.M. Palmer enters the conference room to find his cabinet and Vice President Prescott awaiting him on the video screen. Prescott outlines their intentions – to invoke Section Four of the 25th Amendment to the Constitution, pertaining to the President's inability to continue. Prescott announces that they will be putting the point to a vote, until the Secretary of State points out that some of them are struggling to keep up with events, and Prescott agrees to a discussion, stating he will show evidence of the President's recent erratic behaviour. Palmer shows quite forcibly that he is still in possession of his Presidential faculties, but agrees to the discussion, on one condition. If he comes out of the vote with a majority support, Prescott must tender his resignation as the Vice President of the United States of America. Prescott agrees.

04:15A.M. Tony has received information from a trusted source that the President has called off the attacks. He confronts Chappelle, who knew about the decision. Tony wants to know why his people are still processing intelligence on a dead operation. Chappelle tells him that the order is likely to be reversed by the White House, and CTU should be kept on a war footing.

04:16 A.M. Michelle informs Tony that she has Jack on the line from Kate's house. He quietly asks her to conference the call through to his office. As Jack waits for Tony to come on the line, he attempts to access the chip on a laptop through an adapter, but he is unable to read the data. Jack tells Tony and Michelle that he is unable to read the chip, and Michelle believes she can help. While she prepares, Jack asks Tony to run a background check on Peter Kingsley. Tony informs him that the attack has been called off, but may be reinstated. He doesn't know why, but something is definitely going on in Washington. Ron Wieland is ushered into the Washington conference room, and Prescott announces his credentials. He asks Wieland to outline his experiences at the OC earlier in the day. Wieland reports his incarceration by Secret Service agents after he threatened to release the story about the bomb. Palmer maintains his actions were motivated by the need to protect the public and avoid widespread panic, but Wieland, although agreeing with the President to an extent, believes that under the Bill of Rights, it was his decision to make, not Palmer's. Wieland is excused and Prescott says it will be a few minutes before the next witness is ready.

04:20 A.M. Michelle talks Jack through a sequence that should enable them to read the chip, but all Jack is able to pull up is a series of numbers. He checks the chip, which appears to have been damaged. Michelle tells him to send the data to her screen and she'll attempt to use a retrieval program to find the data. Tony requests the assistance of two IT personnel, and then a call comes through from Kim. Michelle now has the data, but it is highly corrupted. Tony puts Kim through to Jack. She is on her way to the Mathesons' to pick up her things. Kim tells her father how much she misses him and that she just wants to come home now.

04:23 A.M. Palmer asks Novick how long he's known about Prescott's intentions. Novick admits he's known for a couple of hours, and Palmer accuses him of being on Prescott's side all along.

Novick pleads that he's always been on Palmer's side, and asks the President to reconsider his decision, and everything will go away. Palmer, naturally, refuses.

04:29 A.M. Palmer is shocked when Prescott announces his next witness as the unwell Roger Stanton, who appears, pale and tired, on a video screen. Stanton apologises for his condition, having being tortured for several hours by order of the President. Palmer asks him why he was tortured. Stanton believes that the President thought he knew more about the bomb's location than he did, and goes on to relate the events of the day, from Eric Rayburn's dismissal to his torture earlier that evening. He believes the President wanted to avoid war at all costs, even to the extent of convincing himself that Americans may have been responsible. Chappelle confronts Tony as to why he put IT personnel on to a retrieval project. Tony explains that Jack has the chip, albeit damaged, and they are trying to retrieve evidence that will prove the Cyprus recording is a fake.

04:32 A.M. Chappelle calls his own office in order to get a message to the Vice President. Security camera footage of Stanton's torture is played, much to the shock of most of the assembled cabinet members. The footage shows Palmer talking to Stanton, and Stanton finally admitting that the NSA knew about the bomb weeks ago. Palmer has the footage stopped, asserting that Stanton's confession on the video should be enough to halt the meeting. Stanton claims that he broke, and was saying what he thought the President wanted to hear in order to stop the torture. The rest of the footage, of Stanton giving information about the Coral Snake team and Norton Airfield, is missing. There is nobody to confirm what the President is saying as he was the only person present with Stanton at that time. Palmer asks Novick to back him up, but Novick maintains he only knows what the President previously told him. Stanton is dismissed. Prescott offers Palmer the chance to present evidence in his own defence, but the President points out that he's had little time to prepare. As he makes an impassioned speech about halting the attack, Prescott is handed a message from Chappelle, informing them about the possible new information. As the evidence is being reviewed at CTU and could impact on the proceedings, he feels it is necessary to wait.

04:37A.M. Michelle is dismayed when even the IT technicians are unable to configure the data. They have some fragments of information that will be worth following up, but the audio file is missing. Chappelle believes that Bauer has been wasting their time.

The men are led away from Kate's house by the police. Jack finds Kate in the kitchen in a state. She is starting to blame herself for everything that's happened today. She could have stopped Marie becoming a terrorist if only she'd paid her sister more attention. Jack tells her there's nothing she could have done, and they'd never have found the bomb without her. He hugs her, but the moment is broken when Jack's phone rings.

04:42A.M. It is Tony and Michelle on the phone. Jack is annoyed when they tell him that the audio file is missing. Chappelle is calling the President, and he wants Jack conferenced in on the call. Michelle advises Jack that she has found identical code fragments on some of the data remaining on the chip, a sort of hacker's signature. She has traced it back to a programmer named Alex Hewitt, from his FBI file. She gives Jack the address and he leaves Kate's to head over there. Kate tells him to be careful.

04:45A.M. Prescott informs the meeting that the bombers have just refuelled, and if the attack is to go ahead, they must commit to it now. Palmer asks for a few more minutes, and Prescott refers to Jack – everything will be all right once Mr Bauer calls, but it never quite happens. An aide arrives to pass Palmer a phone. Jack and Chappelle are on the line. Jack informs the President that the memory chip was too damaged to access the required evidence, but tells him he is following up a lead on the programmer they believe engineered the Cyprus recording. He also informs him of his run-in with Peter

Kingsley's men, and his belief that the current situation is being manipulated to increase Caspian Sea oil values. Palmer asks him, based on everything he has seen today, if Jack believes the Cyprus recording is a fake. Jack believes it is.

04:47A.M. Palmer informs the assembled cabinet that the evidence is not yet available, but he expects it to be in the very near future. Novick appeals to his friend one last time to authorise the attack, but Palmer is not swayed. He asks for the vote to commence.

04:53A.M. Jack confers with Tony as he arrives at Hewitt's loft apartment, and Tony gives him some background on the programmer. He formerly worked for the State Department, but was caught manipulating files. He has recently attempted suicide while in psychiatric care. Hewitt appears to have no connection to the name Peter Kingsley.

The Secretary of State must cast the deciding vote. Although he believes there is no man more capable of being President of the United States than David Palmer, he feels he must vote against the President. Palmer has the right of appeal in Congress in four days time, but in the meantime he is asked to relinquish his position. He is escorted from the room by Secret Service agents.

04:58A.M. Jack finds the door of Hewitt's apartment unlocked. The place is empty, but has been ransacked. Vice President Prescott is sworn in as President of the United States. As he searches through Hewitt's apartment, Jack is disturbed by the lift arriving. He hides. Two people walk in, one armed with a gun. The second person calls out for Alex and switches on the lights. It is Sherry Palmer. Tick, tick, tick...

CTU INCIDENT REPORT

Haven't I Seen You Somewhere Before?: Maurice Compte (Cole) has guest starred in episodes of *NYPD Blue*, *Chicago Hope*, *Angel* and *Boomtown*. Michael Holden, returning in this episode as Ron Wieland, may be familiar from his recurring role as Joe in *Cheers* between 1989 and 1992. John Rubinstein (Secretary of State) has a career CV as long as your arm, but is best remembered as Harrison Fox Jr in *Crazy Like a Fox*. He has guest starred in everything from *Cannon* to *Star Trek: Voyager*, with a recent recurring role in *Angel* as Linwood Murrow, won Tony awards for his work on Broadway, written novels and composed music for many television series.

Time Checks: At **04:00 A.M.**, Jack makes reference to the bomb going off **five hours** ago. Prescott indicates that the meeting has been called to discuss the erratic behaviour of President Palmer over the past **20 hours**. At **04:15 A.M.**, Tony receives information that the President called off the attack over **an hour** ago. Stanton was arrested just after **06:00 P.M.** Michelle thinks it will take about **15 minutes** to retrieve the data from the chip. Jack refers to being captured and tortured just over **an hour** ago, in case we missed that bit.

Fashion Police: Jack changes clothes for the second time this season, and we have to ask: why? There's also the question of where he got the new threads. Did Kate have a tracksuit top and combat boots that would fit Jack just hanging around the house, or do CTU vehicles come with standard issue kit? It has to be said, he's gone from looking really cool in the suede jacket affair to looking a tad gay once more.

The Perils Of Kim: So *that's* what happened to Kim! Oh Lordy, never have the words 'I'm being taken to the MATHESONS' to pick up my things' had such a ring of menacing inevitability about them. Let's think back – the last we heard, Gary Matheson was on the run for the murder of his wife, so he could pop up at any minute to finish the job he started on Kim. Hang on, 'could'? Um, we'll expect to see Gary about 30 minutes into the next episode.

Still, at least she doesn't have Miguel in the back of the cop car this time, so no chance of any more DIY arson.

It's Not Easy Being Jack: Ooh, he was so close to getting a snog off Kate! Thank god for Michelle Dessler's uncanny knack of timing in ruining the moment. Let's face it, she's the only one who gets to play tonsil tennis in this show, and she doesn't want anyone else to get the limelight. Jack is a little dull this week, his story relegated to mucking about with computers and making puppy-dog eyes at cute blondes. Palmer's 'trial' is much more important than the slushy stuff.

Great Lines:

Prescott: 'I'll apologise if this comes as a surprise, Mr President, but this is a unique situation in the history of our country, calling for unique measures.'

Palmer: 'Let's skip the soundbites and cut to the chase.'

Secretary of State: 'I suggest we all take a few minutes to compose ourselves and then get on with the proceeding.'

Palmer: 'Let's not mince words, Mr Secretary. You mean the trial of David Palmer.'

Stanton: 'David Palmer is a decent man. Maybe he's too decent for the times we live in.'

Death Count: A big fat duck on the death count this week, leaving us in a holding pattern at the big 100.

DEBRIEF

Much of this hour is actually quite a tedious distraction from the matter in hand – the 'trial' of David Palmer. Every second of this sequence was compelling, almost like the climax to a Shakespearean thriller. Prescott makes such a great villain in this sequence, having set up the President for a fall at every turn. The question remains as to whether he's acting for his own ends, but this will surely be answered by the end of the season. Novick's squirming under the gaze of his President is beautiful, and a right royal comeuppance is expected when Palmer regains his office (which surely he will). His ass is so fired!

The reappearance of Sherry Palmer is a welcome surprise, adding some much-needed sauce for the pot at the close of a highly mixed bag of an episode.

Pulse-Rate: 105 bpm

Questions Arising:

- Where is Alex Hewitt?
- What connection does Sherry Palmer have to Hewitt?
- When will Kim start running again?

Production Code: 2AFF22
Written by Virgil Williams and Duppy Demetrius
Directed by Ian Toynton

> *'The following takes place between 5:00A.M. and 6:00A.M.... Events occur in real time.'*

Guest Starring: Reiko Aylesworth (Michelle Dessler), Lourdes Benedicto (Carrie Turner), Billy Burke (Gary Matheson), Jude Ciccolella (Mike Novick), Alan Dale (Vice President Prescott), Paul Schulze (Ryan Chappelle), Glenn Morshower (Agent Aaron Pierce), Rick D. Wasserman (Alex Hewitt), Paco Farias (Deputy Sheriff), Alex Daniels (Bryce), Steven Arthur (Military Officer)

FIELD REPORT

05:00A.M. Jack watches as Sherry sends her bodyguard outside to look for Hewitt. Alone, she begins to look around the apartment. President Prescott confers with a military adviser. Even with the delay caused by the unseating of Palmer, they haven't lost the element of surprise and are able to proceed with the attack as planned. Palmer is being detained and will be kept in custody until after Prescott announces his ascension to office and the US response to the bomb. Novick asks to Palmer to hand over his key codes as they belong to President Prescott. Reluctantly, Palmer hands over the card.

05:04A.M. Chappelle calls all CTU personnel together for a special meeting. Chappelle informs the staff that the cabinet has invoked the 25th Amendment and removed Palmer from office. Tony asks why, but Chappelle says it isn't relevant. Tony disagrees – he believes Palmer was removed because he wanted to wait until all the evidence was in place. Chappelle isn't interested. They work for President Prescott now and Jack Bauer will be given no further assistance from CTU. With the meeting dismissed, Michelle asks Tony what he's going to do. He isn't sure, but wants to speak to somebody on Prescott's team in case Jack does come through with the evidence.

05:06A.M. Sherry's bodyguard returns to the apartment. Hewitt's car is missing. They are about to leave when Jack reveals himself, overcoming the bodyguard immediately. He knocks him unconscious and moves his attention to Sherry. She tells him she is there to help David Palmer, to put her resources into finding out who's behind the bomb. Jack doesn't believe her, and she refuses to answer any more questions. Jack fires a bullet into the wall behind her, which shocks Sherry. She tells Jack that she knows Hewitt was hired by Peter Kingsley to fabricate the Cyprus recording and she knows of his motives behind it. Jack suddenly notices that the bullet hole in the wall has let a stream of light into the room – he fires several times into the wall, ordering whoever is behind the wall to come out. A panel opens and Alex Hewitt walks out. Sherry tells him not to say anything as Jack is a federal agent, but Jack tells her to keep quiet and drags Hewitt away from her for a little chat.

05:14A.M. Jack continues to grill Hewitt, but he will only speak to Sherry as she promised to help him. Jack calls him a traitor, but Hewitt clams up, demanding a lawyer. Jack promises that if Hewitt co-operates, he'll help as much as he can. He points out that the people that Hewitt provided the recordings for would be expecting him to die in the bomb blast, and will now be coming after him. Despite Jack's threats, Hewitt still insists he will only talk to Sherry. Jack locks Hewitt in another room and talks to Sherry. She finally admits that she isn't there to help her ex-husband, she's trying to protect herself. Recordings in Hewitt's possession will incriminate her in the plot to unseat David Palmer. She wanted revenge on her husband, and Kingsley offered her the opportunity, assuring her that the bomb would never go off. Jack starts to phone CTU – Sherry has just confessed to a federal crime, but Sherry demands immunity from any prosecution. Jack needs her to ensure Hewitt's co-operation, and if he doesn't guarantee her immunity, it will be just Jack's word against hers. Jack releases Hewitt and lets him talk to Sherry.

05:19A.M. Palmer asks Agent Pierce if he thinks he's unfit for the position of President. Pierce is under orders not to discuss the situation with Palmer, but that does not prevent him from listening. Palmer makes an impassioned plea that they must have all the evidence before committing to the attack, and if they launch an attack and evidence provided by Jack Bauer disproves the Cyprus recording, they will be at war with three innocent countries. Palmer understands that Pierce has a son in the Navy, and wants to ensure that he will be fighting for a just cause if it comes to it. Pierce agrees to get Palmer a Satphone.

05:21A.M. Carrie is unhappy when Michelle attempts to reassign some of her duties. She thinks Michelle and Tony are still working

with Jack, and tells Tony as much when he asks what's going on. Michelle explains herself, maintaining she is working on something for Division. Not satisfied, Carrie leaves, and both Tony and Michelle know that Carrie didn't believe them. Carrie takes her concerns to Chappelle – she doesn't believe Tony is fit to run CTU.
05:27A.M. Jack calls Tony and is aghast to discover that Palmer has been ousted. He asks for Tony to send over a chopper to pick up Hewitt. He has no doubt that this is the man responsible for the Cyprus recording, and they are working to persuade him to testify. Sherry promises Hewitt immunity from prosecution if he agrees to testify, which he does. Michelle is doubtful as to whether Chappelle will authorise the chopper to pick up Hewitt. Tony doesn't see how Chappelle can ignore what's going on. He informs his superior about Jack's current situation. Chappelle is happy for Hewitt to be brought in, but refuses to authorise a chopper. He advises Tony that he is being reassigned and asks him to clear his desk.
05:31A.M. Hewitt busily prepares to leave, rebuilding files on his computer that have been removed. He's going to demonstrate what he can do by making a recording on the spot and manipulating it in the same way as the Cyprus recording. He then thinks he'll be released, and Jack, with a glance at Sherry, agrees. Hewitt grows suspicious – why is Jack being so nice all of a sudden? He asks to speak to Jack alone, against Sherry's wishes. Hewitt asks Jack if Sherry is about to screw him, but Jack reassures him that she is only trying to help him.
05:39A.M. Jack briefly clutches at his chest in pain. Kim arrives at the Mathesons' house, accompanied by a deputy. The deputy waits for her in the car as she goes inside. After looking at a picture of Megan, she heads upstairs to pack.

Michelle watches as Tony packs up his things, wondering what he's going to do. The phone rings – it is a Satcom call. Tony picks up the phone, surprised to hear David Palmer's voice on the other end. He needs to speak to Jack Bauer. Tony transfers him through to Jack's mobile. Palmer asks Jack what the current situation is, and Jack informs him they have Hewitt in custody and they will bring him in shortly to testify before the cabinet. He also lets Palmer know that his ex-wife is there. Palmer warns Jack not to trust Sherry, and asks to speak to her. Jack hands the phone over. He wants to know why she is there, and she admits that he was right and that the Cyprus audio is a fake. She's only trying to help, but Palmer warns her to stay out of Jack's way. Sherry passes the phone back to Jack. Palmer urges Jack to get Hewitt to them as soon as possible and hangs up. Hewitt has nearly finished his work, and Jack asks Tony for an update on the chopper. He tells him they'll have it.

05:42 A.M. Tony hangs up and turns to Michelle. He needs her help. As Kim packs her things up, she is unaware that Gary Matheson is prowling around outside. Novick enters the room where Palmer is being held and asks for the satphone. Palmer reluctantly hands it over, and Novick asks for Agent Pierce to be taken into custody. Palmer asks that Pierce not be punished, as he coerced the agent into supplying the phone. Novick doesn't believe any coercion was necessary and Pierce is cuffed. Palmer tells Novick he should be ashamed of himself – he should be the one helping him. Palmer apologises to Pierce, who tells him no apology is necessary. As Pierce is led away, another Secret Service agent arrives to take his place. As Kim continues to pack her things, she is unaware that Gary has made his way upstairs, having incapacitated the deputy and taken his weapon. He heads into the bedroom and throws some money and clothes into a bag. Kim hears a noise, and calls out to the deputy, alerting Gary to her presence. She goes to investigate in the Mathesons' bedroom, but nobody is there. She goes back to her own room, and Gary emerges from hiding.

Tony calls Michelle and asks if she's ready. She is. She calls Chappelle and tells him he is needed downstairs. Chappelle heads downstairs, but is confused to find Michelle waiting for him, and even more surprised when Tony grabs him from behind and puts a cloth to his mouth. As Chappelle falls unconscious, Tony tells Michelle to arrange the chopper for Jack. He prepares a syringe.

05:51 A.M. Sherry tells Jack that she's not trying to keep herself clean just for selfish reasons. It wouldn't be good for the President if his ex-wife were implicated in the bomb threat. Sherry is shocked when Jack tells her that Palmer has been unseated by Prescott and she now has what she wanted. Tony calls as he finishes with Chappelle to let him know the chopper is on its way. Jack informs Tony that he's going to have to get the Attorney General involved as Mrs Palmer is going to try to cut a deal. Tony will take care of it. Sherry asks Jack what he meant by saying she was going to 'try' to cut a deal. Hewitt will only testify with her permission and she must have guaranteed immunity. Jack is only concerned with halting the attack – after that, she can cut whatever deal she wants. He prevents her from talking to Hewitt.

05:54 A.M. Kim's bags are packed, and as she leaves her room, she notices the body of the deputy through the window. She starts to run from the house, but Gary sees her and runs after her as she heads into a bedroom. Kim is nowhere to be seen in the bedroom, and Gary pulls down the ladder that leads into the loft. He slowly climbs up, telling Kim this is all her fault. As his head emerges into the loft, Kim smashes him in the face and he falls to the ground, but the ceiling collapses under Kim's weight and she falls on top of him. She isn't badly hurt, and crawls into the corner, grabbing her phone and the gun Gary dropped. With Gary still unconscious, she dials a number.

05:56 A.M. Michelle takes Kim's call as she asks to speak to her dad urgently. Michelle puts her through to Jack. She tells him what has happened and Jack tells Kim to get out of the house. As she gets up, Gary starts to come round. Jack tells Kim to shoot him, but she is scared. He urges her to point the gun at his chest and shoot him. Kim picks up the gun and fires at Gary. Jack tells her to do it again, and Kim grits her teeth, firing once more at Gary. She starts to cry. Jack tells her to go downstairs and he'll phone for somebody to pick her up. As Jack makes to dial a number, Hewitt tries to leave. Things are taking too long, and he doesn't trust Sherry any more. Sherry tells him that people are out to kill him and without their help he won't stand a chance. Jack calls Kate and asks her to go and pick up Kim – the Mathesons' home is in her neighbourhood. She'll call the police and head straight over. Hewitt is trying to leave again, and Jack shouts at him to get back to work. Hewitt stabs Sherry and dives through a concealed hole in the wall. With Sherry lying on the floor bleeding and Hewitt making his escape, Jack has a choice to make. He goes after Hewitt. Tick tick tick...

CTU INCIDENT REPORT

Time Checks: The government has had experts working on the Cyprus recording for the last **six hours**. At **05:31 A.M.**, Chappelle gives Tony **15 minutes** to clear his desk. It will take Hewitt **20 minutes** to rebuild the files removed from his system. At **05:52 A.M.** the chopper should be with Jack in about **20 minutes**.

Behind The Camera: Duppy Demetrius's main role on *24* is to act as assistant to the producers, and he also worked as an uncredited production assistant on *The Pretender*.

Fashion Police: Ooh dear, the continuity police are out in force this week. Kim's hair has grown! Look at it! There's at least an inch on the bottom of that nice bob she had at the start of the season. Tsk tsk. This is very bad, as the production types are usually on the ball with that kind of stuff. Sherry has scrubbed away the layers of make-up she had in the OC sequence, looking a little less Dynasty-era Joan Collins. The bouncy hair and shoulder pads are gone, replaced with comfy and practical togs. She looks altogether less evil – is this significant, we wonder?

The Perils of Kim: Hands up if you were surprised at Gary Matheson's arrival. Nah, didn't think so. To be fair to Kim, this isn't really her fault. You'd think the police might have been staking out the home of a killer on the run in case he came back to pick up some clothes and money. Fools. This episode deserves a special mention for Kim, as we finally get the point of 22 weeks of endless running away when she pops a couple of caps into Gary Matheson's ass. Jack telling her to shoot Gary, turning his daughter into a killer, however necessary, is one of the best character moments in the entire series, and one that was worth all the stupidity along the way. She really is her father's daughter, isn't she?

It's Not Easy Being Jack: Does it look like Jack might be about to keel over from a heart attack? There's just that one moment, very subtly added during a split second in the background as we come back from an ad break, but Jack is definitely clutching his chest in pain. He seems to be losing it a bit at the end of the episode, shouting at everybody, so we can expect him to keel over at exactly the wrong moment – maybe at around **06:59 A.M.**? It's good to see our boy getting back to being good old-fashioned Jack and firing bullets into the wall to scare the crap out of Sherry. Good lad!

Great Lines:
Hewitt: 'I'm not going to say anything else until I talk to a lawyer.'
Jack: 'I am your lawyer, son.'

Sherry: 'I'll handle Agent Bauer, he won't be a problem. He's very low on the food chain.'

Novick: 'I tried to be a friend to you, sir.'
Palmer: 'I don't want a friend. I need someone to do the right thing.'

Death Count: We very nearly had the second duck in a row until Gary Matheson returned to supply the latest cannon fodder for the running tally. With two episodes to go, we currently stand at 101.

DEBRIEF

Oh dear, it's more sitting around in rooms making phone calls this week. Jack just sits around shouting at people and throwing ex-First Ladies on to sofas. Palmer is also locked up, but he does have a comfy chair and a nice widescreen TV to watch. He could just order a big pizza and ask if somebody could run out to Blockbuster and rent him the DVD of *Far From Heaven.*

The best moments this week come from the supporting players. Tony and Michelle take a leaf out of Jack's book and knock their boss unconscious, reminiscent of Jack shooting Mason with a tranq dart way back in **Day One**. We just know that Carrie is going to find Chappelle and blow the whistle. Finally, Kim gets to play a worthwhile chunk of the storyline. It took 22 episodes, but she finally did it!

Pulse-Rate: 100 bpm

Questions Arising:

- ? Is Jack having heart problems?
- ? Will Carrie discover Chappelle's whereabouts?

Production Code: 2AFF23
Written by Gil Grant and Evan Katz
Directed by Jon Cassar

> *'The following takes place between 6:00A.M. and 7:00A.M.... Events occur in real time.'*

Guest Starring: Reiko Aylesworth (Michelle Dessler), Tobin Bell (Peter Kingsley), Lourdes Benedicto (Carrie Turner) Jude Ciccolella (Mike Novick), Thomas Kretschman (Max), Alan Dale (Vice President Prescott), Paul Schulze (Ryan Chappelle), Rick D. Wasserman (Alex Hewitt), Scott Paulin (Brian Jacobs), Randle Mell (Brad Hammond), Nina Landey (Eve), Chuti Tiu (Mae), Tony Wayne (Agent Powers), Heather Salmon (Linda), Miguel Marcott (Prime Minister Of Turkey)

FIELD REPORT

06:00A.M. Michelle has checked on Chappelle – he is still out, but beginning to stir. She advises Tony on the status of the chopper, and he tells her that Carrie is working on other duties, which should distract her. Tony takes a call from Brad Hammond, who demands to know where Chappelle is. Tony is unable to help his suspicious superior, but promises that he'll get Chappelle to call in as soon as he turns up. Jack pursues Hewitt through a network of dark passageways. He shouts out that unless Hewitt allows him to protect him, Peter Kingsley will kill him, but this falls on deaf ears. Hewitt smashes through a window, and Jack pursues him on to the roof of the building. The sun is rising. Hewitt is nowhere in sight.

06:05A.M. Kingsley is in the middle of an acupuncture session (as all good villains should partake of every now and then). He is on the phone to the unseen Max, advising him not to worry. A woman enters carrying a briefcase and he terminates the call. The woman tells him that she retrieved all the recordings and data from Hewitt's loft, but Hewitt had gone. Kingsley is not pleased, and points out that if Hewitt testifies, there'll be nowhere for any of them to hide. Jack spots Hewitt atop another roof, pulling a ladder up after him. Jack runs, but misses the end of the ladder. He has a sudden pain in his chest, but starts to climb up a drainpipe. The chase continues over the rooftops, until Hewitt comes to the edge and can go no further. Jack catches up to him, clutching his chest. Jack shouts that there is nowhere left to run, and Hewitt pulls a gun on him. Jack trains his own gun on Hewitt, and begs him to put the gun down. Just as Hewitt is about to fire, Jack shoots, and hits Hewitt's leg. Hewitt goes over the edge of the roof. Jack climbs down a ladder after him. Hewitt is conscious, but injured. Jack finds blood pouring from a wound at the back of his head. He urges the hacker to hold on for the chopper to arrive.

06:14A.M. Jack puts a call in to Tony to request emergency medical care for Hewitt. The chopper will only be carrying a medical kit, and Jack will have to handle it. Tony also informs Jack that he may not be available from this point on as Chappelle's absence is being noticed. He is sending Michelle out into the field to work from remote access, and he briefs Jack on the channel he can contact her on.

06:15A.M. Tony gives Michelle a keycard that will grant access to the field van. On her way out of the building, Michelle is stopped by Carrie, who is highly suspicious, but Michelle manages to put her off the scent.

06:16A.M. The incarcerated Palmer is paid a visit by his lawyer, Brian, who was assigned to him by the Attorney General. Palmer will have a right to appeal against the decision of the cabinet, but it will take time. Palmer informs Brian about Peter Kingsley's involvement with manipulating the evidence, and asks Brian to find out everything he can about the man. Michelle informs Tony that she is in position in the field van, out in the car park.

06:18A.M. Brad Hammond arrives at CTU with a team from Division. He orders a search of the building to locate Ryan Chappelle, and informs Tony that CTU is being locked down. There is a problem within CTU, and one of Tony's own people alerted them to it. As Hammond proceeds to search for Chappelle, Tony glares at a smug Carrie. Novick speaks to the Vice President, who is urging him to talk to Palmer, but the Chief of Staff doesn't think they'll have much success. Brian comes to see him to advise that Palmer will be appealing and that central to any appeal will be proving that the Cyprus recording is faked. He also mentions that they believe a man called Peter Kingsley is behind the plot. Novick grants access to a computer.

06:20A.M. Carrie accompanies Hammond's agents as they search through the building. They find Chappelle coming round in a locked room. Jack attempts to keep Hewitt talking to keep him awake. He hears the chopper approaching and goes to attract its attention. At CTU, the now awake Chappelle orders the chopper to return to CTU as he will not waste any more resources on Bauer. Jack is aghast when the chopper turns and flies away without setting down. Jack calls Michelle and she tells him that Hammond has locked them down. He demands that she gets the chopper back to them as Hewitt is dying, but there's nothing she can do. When Jack returns to Hewitt, he is indeed dead.

06:28 A.M. Jack calls Michelle to inform her about Hewitt's death and asks her to be ready to interface with his computer when he gets back to Hewitt's loft. Novick speaks with Palmer. They are having problems negotiating a flyover of Turkish airspace for the bombers. The Turkish Prime Minister will only grant the flyover with a personal assurance from the President, and as the handover of power has not yet been announced to the American people, Prescott wants Palmer to do it. Jack arrives back at the loft to find Sherry, still in pain from Hewitt's stab wound. He checks the wound, but it is only superficial and the bleeding has already stopped. Sherry is shocked to discover that Hewitt is dead. Jack tells her they have one chance – to deliver Kingsley. Jack thinks Sherry can set up a fake meeting with him to hand over Hewitt, but Sherry refuses. As Jack gets angry, he is hit with heart pains again. Sherry tells him he needs a doctor, but Jack wants Kingsley first. He tells Sherry that they'll set up a meeting with Kingsley to exchange Hewitt for any evidence he has incriminating her. Without Hewitt, how will they convince Kingsley that this is genuine? Sitting at the computer, Jack says that Hewitt will talk. Kingsley speaks to Max, who we now see on-board a luxury yacht in an unknown location. With the bombers still on course, Hewitt is the last remaining link to the Cyprus recording, and Max urges Kingsley to clean up the loose ends.

Tony is taken into custody at Chappelle's order, who demands to know where Michelle is. Tony maintains he was acting alone, but Carrie believes she'll be working off-site to continue assisting Jack. She thinks she should be able to trace her access code. Tony is taken away to a holding room.

06:34 A.M. From the remote van, Michelle calls Jack, and she takes control of Hewitt's computer. They locate the recording of an earlier conversation between Sherry and Hewitt, and Michelle runs it through to confirm Hewitt's voiceprint. Outside, she spots agents searching the other vans for her. The program confirms they have enough material to manipulate Hewitt's voiceprint, and as Jack locates the program to play back the material, the agents take Michelle into custody.

06:41 A.M. Palmer is ushered into the conference room, having agreed to speak to the Turkish Prime Minister. He insists to Prescott that he has only agreed to help to ensure the safety of the men aboard the bombers. The Turkish Prime Minister is patched through. Kate arrives at the Matheson house to pick up Kim. Kim, in shock, hides from the stranger as she searches through the house, despite Kate calling out her name. She eventually comes out of hiding, still holding Gary Matheson's gun, demanding to know who Kate is. When Kate attempts to explain why she's there, Kim trains the gun on her, but Kate manages to talk her down, and tells her that the sooner they leave, the sooner Kim will be with her dad.

06:45 A.M. Tony and Michelle discuss the charges that Chappelle could bring against them. Tony believes they could push for treason, and says that he will protect Michelle, telling Chappelle that she was just following his orders. Michelle tells Tony that she was acting for what she thought was right, and will stand by her actions side by side with him. Palmer is ushered back into his secure holding room. Novick thanks him for speaking to the Prime Minister, and also tells him that he's granting Palmer access to a low security computer terminal to help him find information on Kingsley. Palmer barely acknowledges his former Chief of Staff, and Novick leaves.

06:52 A.M. Kate drives Kim to CTU. Jack has finished preparing Hewitt's computer terminal, and Sherry begins to dial Kingsley's number.

06:54A.M. Kingsley is surprised to be hearing from Sherry, and even more so when she demands that he hands over all the recordings of their conversations. In return, she'll give him Hewitt. Kingsley asks to speak to Hewitt to verify that she's telling the truth. Jack types a phrase into the keyboard, and Hewitt's voice suddenly speaks from the computer. It is enough to convince Kingsley, who eventually agrees to a meeting at the LA Coliseum. After he terminates the call, he tells the woman he is with that he knows he's being set up, but has no choice but to go. With gunmen set up at the meeting point, Sherry and whoever she is working with won't get out alive. After that, Kingsley will be leaving the country. He thanks the woman and tells her that they'll see each other in Lisbon next week. As they embrace, Kingsley reaches for a knife. As Jack drives himself and Sherry to the meeting point, he suddenly starts to have chest pains again. He blacks out at the wheel and the SUV smashes into a fence and off the road. Tick, tick, tick…

CTU INCIDENT REPORT

Haven't I Seen You Somewhere Before?: German actor Thomas Kretschmann has a lengthy CV of work in his native country, and has guest starred in *Relic Hunter* and *V.I.P.* He played Capt.-Lt Gunther Wassner in *U–571* (2000), Overlord Damaskinos in *Blade II* (2002) and can be seen most recently as Captain Wilm Hosenfeld in the Oscar winning *The Pianist* (2002). As a director, Scott Paulin (Brian Jacobs) has helmed episodes of *Northern Exposure*, *Beverley Hills 90210* and *Dawson's Creek*, among others. As an actor he played Prof. Corey Randall in *Beverley Hills 90210* and has guest starred in *St Elsewhere*, *Chicago Hope* and *Diagnosis Murder.* Nina Landey (Eve) also played the role of Amanda in **Day One** of *24* in the episode **2:00 P.M. – 3:00 P.M.**

Time Checks: At **06:00 A.M.**, the CTU chopper is about **ten minutes** away from Hewitt's loft, meaning that he should be back at CTU in **half an hour**. When Tony speaks to Brad Hammond, Chappelle was noted as arriving at CTU **three hours** ago. Sherry had called Hewitt around **midnight**. At approximately **06:56**, a meeting is set up with Kingsley in **30 minutes** time.

Fashion Police: No real fashion disasters this week, although Kingsley's choice of acupuncture needles have a nice blue colour scheme. Bizarrely.

The Perils Of Kim: Had anyone else almost forgotten about Kim again? The poor girl must have been sitting in that wardrobe for ages waiting for Kate to turn up. The shock of the last 24 hours appears to be getting to her – she has that strange, distant, haunted look in her eyes that Jack has had since **08:00 A.M.** Considering where we are in the story, it's no wonder she was unwilling to trust Kate. Kim in suddenly sensible actions shocker!

It's Not Easy Being Jack: Jack seems to be getting to the point of total exhaustion, which is always good for a laugh, as Kiefer Sutherland plays fatigue so well. His look of pure defeat when Hewitt expires is a signature moment for the entire series, and reflects just how the audience is feeling at this stage. What's the betting that Jack's heart is going to give out at just the wrong moment during the next hour?

Great Lines:

Jack: 'Mrs Palmer, you are going to help me, I'm not going to give you another choice.'

Sherry: 'You wouldn't dare hurt me.'

Jack: 'Make no mistake about it, I will do what I have to do.'

Death Count: The unfortunate Alex Hewitt going for a dive off the roof brings the penultimate death tally up to a respectable 102.

DEBRIEF

As a penultimate episode, this sucks, really. Obviously the production team don't want to show their hand too early, but there's no sense of unbeatable odds coming into play, which the series had in spades at the equivalent point last year. Jack spends most of the episode sitting on rooftops, sitting at computers or sitting in cars, when he really should be running around with a gun doing what Jack does best.

The obvious question of 'will the bombers be stopped in time?' is now what's driving the narrative, which should be enough to push things through to a conclusion in the next hour, but we already know how Jack is going to do it – get Kingsley to admit that the Cyprus recording was faked. It seems entirely probable that he'll succeed (despite certain heart problems), which has removed the suspense and tension element that we so desperately need at this stage. It seems the day peaked with Jack and George's flight of mercy to deliver the bomb in the desert, and the final hour will need a real shot in the arm to reach that height again.

Pulse-Rate: 115 bpm

Questions Arising:

- Where is Max located?
- Why does Kingsley think acupuncture is a good idea?
- Is Hammond working for anyone else?
- Will our heroes manage to avert World War III?

8:00 A.M.

Production Code: **2AFF24**
Story by **Robert Cochran and Howard Gordon**
Teleplay by **Joel Surnow and Michael Loceff**
Directed by **Jon Cassar**

> ***'The following takes place between 7:00A.M. and 8:00A.M.... Events occur in real time.'***

Guest Starring: Reiko Aylesworth (Michelle Dessler), Tobin Bell (Peter Kingsley), Lourdes Benedicto (Carrie Turner), Jude Ciccolella (Mike Novick), Laura Harris (Marie Warner), Thomas Kretschman (Max), John Terry (Bob Warner), Tamlyn Tomita (Jenny Dodge), Alan Dale (Vice President Prescott), Paul Schulze (Ryan Chappelle), Scott Paulin (Brian Jacobs), Eugene Robert Glazer (Alexander Trepkos), Daniel Dae Kim (Agent Tom Baker), Richard Holden (General Stone), Chuti Tiu (Mae), Lilas Lane (Maggie), Fred Saldone (Driver)

FIELD REPORT

07:00A.M. Jack comes round in the stationary vehicle, unharmed but in pain. Sherry has also survived unscathed. Jack attempts to start the van, but the engine is dead. He is unable to leave the vehicle as his seatbelt is jammed. He asks Sherry to help, but she just gets out of the van to leave Jack to his fate. He pleads with her to help him – she's the only one who can, but she simply walks away. Jack can only remain where he is. A few seconds later, Sherry returns, having relented. She begins to cut the seatbelt.

Brian brings Novick a file on Peter Kingsley, showing records of phone calls made by Kingsley to the now deceased Jonathan Wallace.

07:04A.M. A military officer advises President Prescott that the bombers have now flown over their final checkpoint. In a startling about-face, Novick contacts Chappelle and, much to the CTU superior's annoyance and surprise, orders the agency to give Jack Bauer any and all assistance they can in confirming the veracity of the Cyprus recording.

07:06A.M. Kingsley informs Max that he will be en route shortly, but has to take care of Alex Hewitt. Max is unhappy to hear this news, but Kingsley assures him it will be dealt with.

Chappelle enters the holding room where Tony and Michelle await their fate. He asks them how he can get in touch with Jack, and Tony realises what's going on – Chappelle is being squeezed from above as Jack's evidence may have some credence after all. He agrees to help only if Chappelle confirms in writing that the charges against himself and Michelle are dropped. Chappelle reluctantly agrees.

07:08A.M. Jack and Sherry struggle from the crash site. A passing motorist asks them if he can help, and Jack pulls his gun, telling the man that he needs his car. The motorist willingly hands over the vehicle, and Jack and Sherry drive off to their meeting with Kingsley.

07:13A.M. Kate and Kim arrive at CTU and are greeted by the ever-helpful Carrie. She is surprised when Tony arrives to take over, thinking he was still in custody. Tony sends Carrie away and speaks to Kim and Kate. They will get a message to Jack as soon as they are able, but in the meantime, Carrie will look after Kim. Tony tells Kate that her father returned to CTU after his release to speak with Marie, who is being held there. Bob Warner talks to Marie, who is chained up behind a transparent dividing wall. He pleads with her to tell him why she has done these terrible things, just one reason, but Marie remains silent. Kate arrives, telling her father there is no reason. Kate leads him from the room, but Marie calls her back. She tells Kate that she won't be safe out there.

07:17A.M. En route to the meeting point, Jack receives a call from CTU. Tony tells him that Kim is safe, then passes Jack over to Chappelle, who informs Jack that he now has full support from CTU. Jack briefs him on the mission profile. Sherry will be wearing a wire and will attempt to get Kingsley to admit that the Cyprus recording is a fake. He asks for voiceprints of Sherry and Kingsley to be made available for verification, and a direct audio link to the White House. Chappelle agrees.

07:19A.M. Jack and Sherry arrive at the rendezvous point. Jack fits Sherry with the wire – they are ready to go.

07:24A.M. Novick contacts President Prescott to advise him that it's likely they'll soon be receiving conclusive evidence that the Cyprus recordings are false. He briefs the President on Jack's current situation and that they are expecting a full confession from Kingsley. Michelle has set up the computer for voice print verification, and confirms that Sherry Palmer is present with Jack. Chappelle thinks they should wait for back-up, but Jack tells him they don't have time. They are good to go.

07:26A.M. As Jack experiences further pain, Sherry makes her way into the building. Before she leaves, she tells Jack that she's doing this for David. Palmer is shown into the conference room. Novick briefs him on the situation, and that he and Prescott thought it would be best to have Palmer present at the sting operation against Peter Kingsley. Palmer reacts badly when he discovers it will be his ex-wife in the middle of the action and that she was part of the original plot to detonate the bomb. Sherry makes her way into the Coliseum as a sniper takes position above her.

07:34A.M. Kingsley arrives and his armed men fan out around the building. Jack takes his own position with the audio equipment. Kingsley has arrived at Sherry's position and searches her, but doesn't find the wire. He asks where Hewitt is, and Sherry replies that he's safe. She keeps him talking to allow CTU to verify that this is Peter Kingsley – Michelle confirms the voiceprint match. Sherry is asking for safe haven in return for Hewitt, which Kingsley is unhappy about. She also asks for all recordings, including the Cyprus source recordings, pertaining to the bomb, for her own insurance. She manages to manipulate Kingsley into admitting that the recording was faked, and the White House has the proof it needed. Jack wants to pull her out of there now.

07:37A.M. Sherry tells Kingsley that she'll call him with Hewitt's location as soon as she is safe, but he knows she is bluffing and doesn't have Hewitt. Kingsley orders the sniper to shoot her, but when a bullet fails to come, he realises that his man has been taken out and orders one of his ground operatives to kill her. Jack begins shooting from the sniper's position and shouts for Sherry to run. Kingsley takes cover. Having emptied the rifle cartridge, Jack leaves his position and runs to find Sherry. Running through the inside of the building, the pair are waylaid by one of Kingsley's remaining men, and Jack orders Sherry to get out of there as he takes on the man. After a drawn out fight, Jack despatches his attacker, but the exertion has caused more damage to his heart and he collapses. Kingsley approaches the prone Jack, gun drawn. Jack scrabbles for a discarded gun, but is unable to reach it. As Kingsley raises his gun to fire, a CTU chopper flies overhead and Kingsley is taken out. As the SWAT team moves in on his location, Jack loses consciousness.

07:42A.M. The bombers are minutes away from their target, and General Stone looks to Prescott for orders. He orders the bombers to abort their mission.

07:47 A.M. Aboard his yacht, Max speaks on the phone with Trepkos, who tells him that Kingsley is dead and the bombers have aborted their mission. There will be no war. Max tells Trepkos that they will have to do this another way, and it will begin today. He makes another call and tells the person at the other end to go ahead.

Prescott hands back the Presidency to Palmer, and tenders his resignation, along with those of the members of the cabinet who voted against him. Palmer refuses the resignations, and makes an impassioned speech about the work they have to do. He asks Jenny to set up a press conference as soon as possible, before asking Novick for his resignation.

07:52 A.M. Tony enters his office to find Chappelle still there. As Chappelle basks in the glory of success, Tony asks him to get out of his chair. Chappelle leaves, and Michelle comes to tell Tony that the new shift has arrived and she's heading home. He thanks her for her help and the choices she made today. She starts to leave, and Tony tells her he'll see her tomorrow. She breaks into a wide grin as she heads down the steps, and we finally see Tony smile as he goes back to his desk.

07:54 A.M. Kim and Kate arrive at the Coliseum, where Kim is reunited with her father, who is being given medical attention. She tells Jack that she'll take care of him from now on, and Jack falls asleep in her arms with Kate looking on, a smile on her face.

After giving his statement to the public, Palmer makes his way through the crowds, shaking hands with well-wishers. A dark-haired girl makes her way through the crowds towards him, desperate to shake his hand. The President clasps her hands for a few seconds before moving on.

Sherry Palmer is led away in handcuffs. Carrie and Chappelle leave CTU. Jack is loaded into an ambulance. The dark-haired girl walks away from the crowds, and in a secluded spot, pulls a transparent strip off her hand with a pair of tongs. She places the strip in a secure container, and phones Max to tell him it's done.

Palmer is still waving to the crowds when he collapses to the ground, his hand scarred and blotchy. He loses consciousness. Tick, tick, tick...

CTU INCIDENT REPORT

Haven't I Seen You Somewhere Before?: Eugene Robert Glazer (Alexander Trepkos) worked for *24*'s creators previously in the regular role of Paul L. Wolfe (aka Operations) throughout the entire run of *La Femme Nikita*. Amongst Richard Holden's (General Stone) early work is an appearance in the classic BBC costume saga *Poldark*, playing 'Jury Foreman'.

Time Checks: Kingsley's last calls to Jonathan Wallace were made as little as **six hours** ago. As of **07:04 A.M.**, the bombers will be reaching their target within the hour (lucky, what with this being the last episode!). At **07:06 A.M.**, Peter Kingsley confirms he'll be on a plane within the hour. He must be expecting his meeting with Sherry to go *very* quickly. At **07:24 A.M.**, Novick tells Prescott that they may have new evidence in the next **half hour**. At **07:25 A.M.**, the bombers are less than **20 minutes** away from their targets. The CTU back-up squad for Jack is **11 minutes** away at **07:26 A.M.**

Fashion Police: Kingsley was doing so well in the well-turned-out villain stakes. He had a neatly trimmed goatee, nicely cut suit and regular acupuncture. Then it all goes horribly wrong in the final reel. He changes into a pair of jeans that, frankly, could have been picked up at Matalan for twenty quid, and combines them with a bad tan suede jacket. It makes his super villain's snarling at Jack about as effective as the British government's locating of weapons of mass destruction.

The Perils Of Kim: Two for two! For the second consecutive episode, Kim manages to get through an hour without putting a foot out of line, to make it to Elisha Cuthbert's second and final scene with Kiefer Sutherland in the entire series. Kimberley, you have provided hours of entertainment throughout this second day of almost real-time action, and we pray with all our hearts that you'll be back to run another day for **Day Three**.

It's Not Easy Being Jack: Flying in the face of what this category stands for, Jack has quite an easy time of it this hour. Apart from chronic heart pains that threaten to kill him at any moment. He listens to Sherry on his walkman for a few minutes, picks off Kingsley's men easily, breaks another man's neck and lies down to defeat the villain at the end before getting a cosy gurney to lie on. It's certainly a far cry from having your wife bleed to death in your arms. Oh, but if Kim stays true to her promise that she's going to look after her old dad from now on, nuclear bombs, international terrorists, World War III and the woman who killed his wife are going to be the least of his worries. Run away, Jack, run far, far away!

Great Lines:

Sherry: 'You're a very impressive man, Jack, but you see everything as either good or bad, just like David, and the world is so much more complicated than that.'

Jack: 'No, it's simple! There's a war about to start, and you're the only person who can help me stop it!'

Marie (to Kate): 'You think you'll be safe out there? You won't be.'

Palmer: 'We came dangerously close to war today. That we all have reacted emotionally to the nuclear detonation is understandable. But leaders are required to have patience beyond human limits.

> The kind of action we nearly took should only be exercised after all other avenues have been exhausted, after the strictest standard of proof has been met. By casting me aside so quickly, you effectively lowered those standards, and that was a profound mistake.'

Tony (to Chappelle): 'Either fire me, or get out of my chair.'

Death Count: A nearly death-free final episode was pulled back from the brink by Jack's judicious pruning of Kingsley's men with the sniper's rifle. Including Kingsley, that makes seven deaths (assuming that horrible crunching noise was Jack breaking his attacker's neck), giving us a final count of 108 deaths throughout 24 episodes. Fact fans may be interested to know that makes an average of 4.5 deaths an episode.

Trivia: It's nice to know that CTU purchases safe vehicles for the use of field agents. Although we don't see this happen on-screen, the driver's airbag has discharged during the SUV's trip off the road. Remember, clunk-click, every trip!

DEBRIEF

Phew! Where to start? In true *24* style, the show manages to provide a final episode that, while being as thoroughly entertaining as always, doesn't quite satisfy in the way that the previous highpoints of the day have.

Everything feels far too easy as a resolution to the day, as noted in the Debrief for the previous hour, and then it becomes apparent as to exactly why that is. The whole point of this final episode is to deliver a cliffhanger from nowhere and set up plot strands for **Day Three**, which had been commissioned a few months before the final episodes were shot.

The most satisfying moments of the episode are reserved for the supporting players. Tony and Michelle get to stick it to Chappelle and Carrie when they hand out the humble pie for consumption. Tony manages to snatch a contender for Best Moment of the Day when he tells Chappelle to get out of his chair, although the dear departed George Mason walks away with that award for his dedication to wry one-liners. Also of note is the 'Oh shit!' expression on Prescott's face when he realises he's made the biggest mistake of his political life. Priceless.

However, so much has been left hanging, no doubt to be revisited in **Day Three**. Marie Warner seems to know more of what is to come, with her chilling proclamation to Kate. Speaking of Kate, she didn't get that snog with Jack, so it's a safe bet she'll be popping in next year, and the secret of Bob Warner's goatee beard has yet to be uncovered.

Fan reaction to the cliffhanger ending was mixed, with most comments leaning towards a sense of being cheated. As last year was resolved quite nicely, it can be frustrating to have loose ends trailing, but this forgets the tradition of the uncertain ending in US TV. Can we ever forget JR Ewing being gunned down? Fox Mulder inside a railroad car as it went up in smoke? Captain Picard appearing on the screen of the *Enterprise* covered in Borg implants and declaring that resistance was futile? All classic moments of great TV, and David Palmer lying unconscious on the ground is another to add to the list. But, beyond the cliffhanger, the big surprise here was the identity of the assassin – **Day One**'s plane-blowing-up, leather-clad terrorist for hire, Mandy. She was last seen riding off into the distance, having being offered a job by Ira Gaines for the summer. Was that job connected to Max and the oil consortium? Will the plot of **Day One** have more impact on Jack's life for **Day Three**? And has Palmer's route to the White House been manipulated from the very beginning? While the cliffhanger may be somewhat unsatisfactory, the return of Mandy adds a welcome dimension to the proceedings.

One thing is certain. Whatever we thought of the ending, we'll all be back next year. How on earth do they top that? I can't wait to find out!

Pulse Rate: 120 bpm

Questions Arising:

- What happened to Lynne Kresge?
- Will Sherry Palmer cut a deal to gain her freedom?
- Was Prescott just misguided or acting for the bad guys all along?
- Will Tony and Michelle get it together?
- How does Max hope the attempt on Palmer's life will change the situation in his consortium's favour?
- What is Mandy's involvement with Max and the oil consortium?
- Is Palmer dead?
- Will Jack be able to return to CTU as a full-time agent or will his heart disallow him from returning to active service?
- What now?

Appendix

Awards and Nominations 2002

Television Critics Association Awards

New Programme of the Year – Winner

Programme of the Year – Winner

Individual Achievement in Drama (Kiefer Sutherland) – Nominated

Outstanding Achievement in Drama (Programme) – Nominated

Motion Picture Sound Editors, USA

Golden Reel Award for Best Sound Editing – Dialogue
(Episode **12:00A.M. – 1:00A.M.**) – Nominated

Golden Satellite Awards

Best Performance by an Actor in a Drama Series
(Kiefer Sutherland) – Winner

Best Television Drama Series – Winner

Golden Globes

Best Performance by an Actor in a Television Series
(Kiefer Sutherland) – Winner

Best Television Drama Series – Nominated

Emmy Awards

Outstanding Single Camera Picture Editing (**7:00A.M. – 8:00A.M.**) – Winner

Outstanding Writing for a Drama Series (Joel Surnow & Robert Cochran for **12:00A.M. – 1:00A.M.**) – Winner

Outstanding Art Direction for a Single Camera Series – Nominated

Outstanding Casting for a Drama Series (Debi Manwiller & Richard Pagano) – Nominated

Outstanding Directing for a Drama Series (Stephen Hopkins) – Nominated

Outstanding Drama Series – Nominated

Outstanding Lead Actor in a Drama Series (Kiefer Sutherland) – Nominated

Outstanding Music Composition (Sean Callery) – Nominated

Outstanding Single Camera Picture Editing (David B. Thompson) – Nominated

Outstanding Single Camera Sound Mixing – Nominated

Directors Guild of America

Outstanding Directorial Achievement in Dramatic Series – Night (Stephen Hopkins) – Nominated

Casting Society of America

Artios Award for Best Casting for TV (Richard Pagano, Debi Manwiller, Peggy Kennedy) – Nominated

Artios Award for Best Casting for TV Pilot (Debi Manwiller) – Nominated

Art Directors Guild

Excellence in Production Design Award (Carlos Barbosa) – Nominated

American Society of Cinematographers

ASC Award for Outstanding Cinematography (Peter Levy – **Pilot**) – Nominated

American Cinema Editors

Eddie Award for Best Edited One-Hour Series (Chris G. Willingham – **4:00A.M. – 5:00A.M.**) – Nominated

ALMA Awards

Outstanding Supporting Actor in a Television Series (David Barrera) – Nominated

2003

Screen Actors Guild Awards

Outstanding Performance by a Male Actor (Kiefer Sutherland) – Nominated

Outstanding Performance by an Ensemble (Cast) – Nominated

PGA Golden Laurel Awards

Television Producer of the Year in Episodic (Brian Grazer, Tony Krantz, Howard Gordon, Robert Cochran, Joel Surnow, Cyrus Yavneh) – Winner

Motion Picture Sound Editors, USA

Golden Reel Award for Best Sound Editing – Dialogue (Episode **10:00A.M. – 11:00A.M.**) – Nominated

Image Awards

Outstanding Actor in a Drama Series (Dennis Haysbert) – Nominated

Outstanding Drama Series – Nominated

Golden Satellite Awards

Best Performance by an Actor in a Drama Series (Kiefer Sutherland) – Winner

Best Performance by an Actress in a Supporting Role in a Drama Series (Sarah Clarke) – Winner

Best Performance by an Actor in a Supporting Role in a Drama Series (Dennis Haysbert) – Nominated

Best Television Drama Series – Nominated

Golden Globes

Best Performance by an Actor in a Television Series (Kiefer Sutherland) – Nominated

Best Performance by an Actor in a Supporting Role (Dennis Haysbert) – Nominated

Best Television Drama Series – Nominated

Cinema Audio Society

CAS Award for Outstanding Sound Mixing (**11:00A.M. – 12:00P.M.**) – Nominated

American Cinema Editors

Eddie Award for Best Edited One-Hour Series (Chris G. Willingham – **2:00P.M. – 3:00P.M.**) – Nominated

Academy of Science Fiction, Fantasy & Horror Films

Cinescape Genre Face of the Future Award (Sarah Wynter) – Nominated

Internet Sites

As with any TV series that attracts a huge cult audience, a thriving online community has sprung up devoted to the series. Here are some of the websites you should take a look at for more information on the fact and fiction behind *24*.

Official Fox Website

[www.fox.com/24]

With the full resources of Fox behind it, the first and, honestly, best place to go is the official site. This is a beautifully designed site, updated once a week during the show's run. Here you will find a full episode guide for both Days, with a detailed synopsis for each hour, broken down into straight plot, or character specific moments. Other features include a recently added Script to Screen section.

Official BBC Site

[www.bbc.co.uk/24]

Very similar in content to the Fox site, this site complements the BBC's run of the show. In addition to the episode guide, you will find actor biographies and details of BBC 3's *Pure 24*, the regular discussion show devoted to the series. You will also find a very busy message board here, split between spoilers and non-spoilers. If you post anything containing a future plot point on the spoiler-free variety, expect a stern telling-off from the moderator – and quite right too!

The Internet Movie Database

[www.imdb.com]

How we lived without imdb.com before the invention of the Internet is anybody's guess. A ridiculously useful online resource that pulls together information on practically every film and television show ever made, alongside comprehensive biographies and filmographies for actors living and dead. This is the place to find out more about the various guest stars that populate a series of *24*. Highly recommended.

Television Without Pity

[www.televisionwithoutpity.com]

An indispensable site devoted to just about every U.S. TV show currently in production. Regular correspondents post wittily observed and very funny synopses of every episode that can often be more entertaining than watching the series themselves. Good fun.

Yahoo!Groups

[www.yahoogroups.com]

If you fancy dipping your toes into the world of online fan discussion about *24*, then look no further than Yahoo!Groups. Various groups have popped up here devoted to the show, but the two best are TwentyFour (http://groups.yahoo.com/group/TwentyFour/) and 24 (http://groups.yahoo.com/group/24/), which are busy places with plenty of discussion. Just make sure you know your netiquette.

The 24 Drinking Game

As a bit of fun to accompany you on those long block viewings of entire seasons of *24*, you may like to partake of a small tipple with this handy drinking game. Thanks to actor Lennie James who helpfully provided the idea after a recording of *Pure 24* in Manchester. Naturally, as drinking can seriously damage your health, we don't recommend you do this very often.

- Whenever Jack says 'The following takes place between…', take a sip.
- Whenever the clock appears on screen, take a sip.
- When there's a split-screen moment, take a sip.
- Whenever anyone mentions how long something will take, or a time check, take a sip.
- Whenever Tony stares at somebody over a computer monitor, take a sip.
- Whenever Mason has funny line, take a gulp.

- Whenever Palmer takes a pause in the middle of a sentence, take a sip.
- Whenever Kim starts running, take a sip.
- Whenever Kim does something stupid, take a gulp.
- Whenever Kim does something that you'd also do when faced with that situation, drain your glass (guaranteed never to get you drunk).
- Whenever Jack repeats anything twice into a walkie talkie, take a gulp.
- If somebody says 'A bomb is going to go off in LA sometime today!', take a gulp.
- When Jack and Kim share a scene together, drain your glass.
- When the bomb goes off, drain your glass.
- When the closing credits of the last episode roll, drain the bottle.

The Final Word

Phew! That's that. Another 24 hours (well, 16.4 hours if you want to be picky and cut out the ad breaks) of thrills and spills, red herrings and double dealings, all wrapped up in one of the most ridiculously entertaining series to hit our screens in years.

As early as February 2003, Fox announced that a third season of *24* would be entering production over the summer, based on the massively improved ratings for the new season. **Day One** had attracted an average rating of 8.6 million viewers, which rose to just over 11 million viewers throughout **Day Two**, proof of *24*'s growing popularity. Similarly improved ratings in the UK were also cause for celebration. Naturally, questions and gossip began to circulate the moment that Fox executive Gail Berman made the announcement.

It's difficult to cut the wheat from the chaff in the midst of so much scuttlebutt, and when the tabloids report that Kiefer Sutherland has signed a $10 million deal for six more seasons, and that the show will be returning as a movie, some hefty pinches of salt are needed along the way.

What is known at this stage is that both Kiefer Sutherland and Sarah Wynter have been issued with contracts for the third season, adding fuel to the fire that Jack and Kate may get it together. It also seems likely that we'll see the return of Carlos Bernard, Reiko

Aylesworth, Elisha Cuthbert, and Paul Schulze. The big question mark hangs over the fate of President Palmer, and Dennis Haysbert is being as cagey as the producers, maintaining that he doesn't know yet if he'll be back.

Other rumours indicate that after the world-shattering events of **Day Two**, the third season will take a more personal look at Jack's life, while maintaining the real-time aspect that has made the show the critical and now ratings success that it is. Whether or not **Day Three** will pick up from where **Day Two** left off isn't known, but hopefully they'll allow Jack to get some sleep. Gail Berman has also indicated that the return of Mandy in the closing minutes of **Day Two** will not be the driving plot behind the next season, but the character will certainly be involved.

The main question on everybody's mind though is: 'How?'

24: Day Three is scheduled to kick off in the U.S. on Tuesday 21 October 2003. Book your place at the water cooler now!